W9-BUZ-450

OBJECTIVISM IN ONE LESSON

An Introduction to the Philosophy of Ayn Rand

Andrew Bernstein

Hamilton Books
A member of
The Rowman & Littlefield Publishing Group
Lanham · Boulder · New York · Toronto · Plymouth, UK

Copyright © 2008 by
Hamilton Books
4501 Forbes Boulevard
Suite 200
Lanham, Maryland 20706
Hamilton Books Acquisitions Department (301) 459-3366

Estover Road
Plymouth PL6 7PY
United Kingdom

All rights reserved
Printed in the United States of America
British Library Cataloging in Publication Information Available

Library of Congress Control Number: 2008933999
ISBN-13: 978-0-7618-4359-7 (paperback : alk. paper)
ISBN-10: 0-7618-4359-0 (paperback : alk. paper)
eISBN-13: 978-0-7618-4360-3
eISBN-10: 0-7618-4360-4

∞™ The paper used in this publication meets the minimum
requirements of American National Standard for Information
Sciences—Permanence of Paper for Printed Library Materials,
ANSI Z39.48—1984

To Penelope Joy,

Who Has a Brilliant Future Ahead of Her

Contents

Preface

Ayn Rand's novels are beloved by the American people and by many others around the world. *The Fountainhead* and *Atlas Shrugged*, for example, have each sold millions of copies and continue to sell well over 100,000 copies annually, decades after their publications. Because of their brilliant plot structures and vivid characterizations, these books are widely read and admired. As millions of readers have discovered, Ayn Rand wove her revolutionary philosophy of Objectivism inextricably into the plots, characters, and actions of these novels, suffusing them with a rare intellectual depth.

Ayn Rand wrote many non-fiction books and essays, as well, but no comprehensive theoretical presentation of her philosophy. The definitive treatment of her thought is Leonard Peikoff's *Objectivism: the Philosophy of Ayn Rand (OPAR)*. Dr. Peikoff, Ayn Rand's leading student and long-time associate, wrote an in-depth work in philosophy that is ideal for advanced students; but it was never intended as an introduction to Objectivism. Consequently, a bridge is needed, an introductory text for the millions of readers who love Ayn Rand's novels and who want to take the next step in understanding her philosophy that will culminate with their study of *OPAR*.

Objectivism in One Lesson is that text.

This book therefore assumes that the reader has some familiarity with Ayn Rand's novels—especially *Anthem, The Fountainhead*, and/or *Atlas Shrugged*—and now seeks to further explore Ayn Rand's distinctive ideas.

Some readers will be familiar with Henry Hazlitt's *Economics in One Lesson*, a book that served, in part, as inspiration for this one. Hazlitt's excellent little book explained the fundamentals of economics by reference to one principle—the necessity to identify *all* consequences of an economic action on *all* individuals, not merely some effects on some people. Hazlitt brilliantly showed the beneficial effects of observing this principle, and the deleterious results of repudiating it.

In a similar manner, this book seeks to show that Ayn Rand's philosophy, on every question, topic, and issue, from its commitment to logic to its advocacy of selfishness to its championing of laissez-faire capitalism, to every other, is integrated around one unifying theme: *man's rational mind is his sole means of gaining knowledge, survival, and happiness*. This, as will be seen, is: The Lesson of Objectivism. If human beings recognize and follow this principle, we will flourish. If we deny or ignore it, we will act as our own destroyers.

Acknowledgements

The author wishes to thank many people for their help in making this book possible.

Numerous experts in Ayn Rand's philosophy provided invaluable editorial support in the book's preparation. Dr. Onkar Ghate, the book's primary editor, spent long hours of work in helping to greatly improve the manuscript. Dr. Yaron Brook read the completed manuscript and provided critical feedback—as did Dr. Michael Berliner.

Jessie Doby and Cory Baron performed invaluable work to get the manuscript ready.

Businessman and raconteur extraordinaire, Sidney Gunst, helped fund the writing. My literary agent, the ball of coruscating energy known as Holly White, as always, has supported this project in numerous ways. Also as always, my beautiful daughter, Penelope Joy, now aged five, provides her daddy hope in a better future than mankind's past.

Above all, the literary and philosophical genius of Ayn Rand must be acknowledged. Her ideas can and will change the world immensely for the better.

Chapter 1

Why Philosophy?

Objectivism is a full system of philosophical thought.

But what is philosophy?—a discerning reader might ask. And why should I bother with the subject at all? Many people don't know clearly what philosophy is, or, even if they have some conception of the subject, think it is a field of esoteric abstractions unrelated to daily life.

But in fact, philosophy is the most practical subject of all—that is, if what one seeks to *practice* is a flourishing human life.

The reason is that philosophy asks and answers life's most fundamental and important questions, those issues regarding which every individual and society need wisdom: What kind of world do we live in? What kind of being is man— and therefore what kind of being am I? By what means do we gain knowledge? What is good for us and what is evil? What type of political system best promotes human life and happiness?

To illustrate this point, imagine several young men growing up in different families, in varying locales, readying to leave their childhood homes and make their respective ways in the world.

One youth, from a rural background, let us say, did not learn to speak until age four, and, when five, was whipped by his father for setting fire to the barn in order to "see what would happen." He received a grand total of three months of formal education, dropping out at age seven when the headmaster pronounced him "addled." - rotten / stupid

But he studied voraciously at home. Although lacking proficiency in mathematics, he excelled at chemistry and mechanics, performed sophisticated experiments, and filled his parents' basement with wire, chemicals, and abandoned pieces of machinery. He was working at age twelve and departed his family's home for independent life by sixteen. traveling

He worked for years as an itinerant employee of the telegraph company, wandering from one Midwestern town to another. But he continued his autodi-

self-taught

1

dactic studies, educating himself regarding the principles of electricity by means of a "driving determination" to overcome all obstacles. His brilliantly creative brain was a fount of original ideas. He immensely improved both the telegraph and telephone—and then invented a device totally new: the phonograph. Soon after, he embarked on the most audacious undertaking of his burgeoning career: an attempt to create a feasible incandescent electric light.

It was a daunting venture. The field's leading experts believed that any lighting system employing incandescence was incapable of success. A rival inventor proclaimed that such an attempt was doomed to "final, necessary and ignominious failure." The main problems—the production of a continuous glow, its possible distribution, and its effective supply of current—had never been solved. But our determined young man, still only in his thirties, believed that genius was "one percent inspiration and ninety-nine percent perspiration." Indefatigably, he stayed at it; in time, he solved them all.

The first youth of this illustration—Thomas Edison—went against received opinion among electrical engineers. Where they held that the electric light required high voltage and low resistance, he was first to understand that such illumination would necessarily employ low voltage and high resistance. He invented the first electric light. He went on to create a power plant and a full lighting system. When the great English scientist, William Thomson (Lord Kelvin), was asked why nobody else had created incandescent lighting, he replied tersely: "The only answer I can think of is that no one else is Edison."

What philosophic principles are involved in Edison's life and achievements? Whether he held them explicitly or implicitly, in conscious intellectual terms or only as nascent, partially formed ideas, what were his theories of reality, knowledge, man, virtue, and society?

Although Edison read widely and learned from earlier geniuses, such as Isaac Newton and Michael Faraday, he never forgot that even they might be mired in preconceived dogma and its associated error. Consequently, he "proved all things to himself through his own method of objective examination and experimentation." His theory regarding the means of human knowledge is clear: we start with the direct observation of facts—and then question, experiment, and theorize in the attempt to explain such facts. Observation- based rationality, rather than faith in the supernatural or slavish obedience to emotional desires, is the method by which men learn. Above all, the independent use of his own mind, rather than uncritical conformity to the convictions of others, is the means by which man gains knowledge of life's fundamental truths.[1]

Such a theory of knowledge intimately involves a corresponding theory of reality: the universe is held to be a place governed by natural law in which events are orderly and necessitated by antecedent causal factors. There are no miracles or violations of nature's lawfulness: burning bushes do not speak, virgins do not give birth, and tigers never spring forth as a result of flinging rose seeds upon the ground. It is a secular, rather than a religious or supernatural theory of the universe—a world in which an entity is what it is—is not what it is not—and consequently acts in accordance with its nature. Such a world—and only such a world—is knowable by application of man's reason.

What type of being is man? Edison—or a person like him—necessarily holds that human beings are capable of great achievement, that rational thinking and indefatigable effort are the means, and that exalted positive, life-promoting accomplishments are the result. The human individual, by means of rational thought and unstinting exertion, can face and overcome daunting obstacles and thereby rise to a level of significant heroism.

Regarding virtue, such a life embodies the conviction that moral goodness lies in commitment to the values that one loves, to self-actualization, to accomplishing, never surrendering or sacrificing one's main purposes. If a man values things that, in fact, advance human life on earth—such as technological invention or art or medicine or business productivity or family and children, etc.—then he should fill his life with those things and/or persons. It is right for him to pursue his own happiness, and to never betray his precious loves or goals. He should fulfill, rather than sacrifice the self.

Politically, on this view, a proper society is one in which an individual's "inalienable right" to self-actualize is acknowledged and legally protected. If a man is to pursue his own vision—as Edison, par excellence, did—then he must be politically and economically free to do so, rather than being enslaved to church or state. A political theory of individual rights, limited Constitutional government, and political-economic freedom is logically embodied in the life of such a self-made man as Edison, rather than one of selfless service to God or Society.

Most human beings are not extraordinary geniuses like Edison—but any individual, who, by means of his own mind and effort, rises in the world, in any productive field, lives out the same basic philosophy, whether consciously articulated or merely felt implicitly at the emotional level.

But whether human beings hold their fundamental ideas consciously or subconsciously, implicitly or explicitly, they at times disagree widely regarding these ideas. For example, a second young man's life unfortunately illustrates an entirely different philosophy.

He was born during the height of Edison's success in the late 19th century—but was urban, not rural, growing up in Brooklyn, New York. His father, an Italian immigrant, was a successful barber, opening and operating his own shop—and was fully literate. They were a conventional immigrant family, initially poor, living in a cold water tenement flat near the Brooklyn Navy Yard. The father was close to his children, taking time to talk to them, sometimes preaching, but never striking them. The family was described as "subdued," lacking any spectacular vices. The neighborhood was an ethnic mixture of Irish, Germans, Italians, Swedes, and Chinese.

The young man went to public schools where discipline was strict and prejudice against Italian immigrants severe. Nevertheless, he was intelligent and diligent and did well, earning straight "Bs" until the 6th grade. However, at age 14 he lost his temper at a teacher, she struck him, he hit her back—and he was expelled, never again to attend school.

After his expulsion, he went to work, laboring faithfully in a factory and later as a paper cutter for six years, helping to support his family. According to those who knew the family, there were no stories of this young man practicing with guns; rather, it was said that he went home each night to his mother.

Unfortunately, he also chose to run errands for a local mobster named Johnny Torrio, a so-called "gentleman gangster" visible as a numbers runner but incognito as a behind-the-scenes owner of brothels and other sleazy rackets. Torrio moved to Chicago and eventually the smart young man caught the eye of Frankie Yale, a strong-arm Brooklyn thug who hired him to tend bar at the Harvard Club on Coney Island. At the bar, the young man "praised" an attractive woman with a vulgar comment, causing her brother to punch him. The youth became enraged and the brother pulled a knife, slashing the young man's face three times. The wounds healed but long, ugly scars remained, engendering his infamous nickname of "Scarface." The brother spoke to the notorious mobster Lucky Luciano who spoke to Frankie Yale. The result was a meeting between the four men in which the gangsters demanded an apology from the young man. Afterwards, Frankie Yale taught him the brutal methods of a thug able to escape justice.

Still, the young man had an opportunity for an honest life. At age 19, he met and fell in love with a respected middle class Irish woman two years his senior named Mae Coughlin. After she had a baby, they married, and he quit Yale's employ, taking a job as an accountant for a legitimate construction firm in Baltimore. He was smart, reliable, and had a head for figures, and for a while the young family flourished. But a year later, after the death of his hard-working father, he veered fatefully and finally back toward crime. At age twenty-two, accepting an offer from Johnny Torrio, Alphonse "Al" Capone moved to Chicago to "work" in the rackets under his former boss.

Eventually, Capone became the criminal "czar" of Cicero, Illinois and a major figure in bootlegging and other Chicago rackets. In the end, he was convicted in federal court and died of syphilis after years of incarceration at Alcatraz.

What were the ideas held by this man that impelled him to a life of crime and murder? Before answering this question it is instructive to note that he did not come from a broken family, did not suffer under an alcoholic, violent father, and did not lack for education, love, or career opportunities. Clearly, he chose the "career" he embarked on from a range of diverse possibilities. (Indeed, his older brother, James Vincenzo Capone, joined the Army during World War I and served with the American Expeditionary Force in France, rising to the rank of Lieutenant. After the war, he moved out west and, ironically, became a Prohibition officer in Nebraska. At one time he was a bodyguard for President Calvin Coolidge, and worked as an honest and effective lawman for several decades.)[2]

It must be understood that although a gangster might be intelligent and (briefly) a competent accountant, he does not seek knowledge by rational thought. Rather, his *desires* are treated as his primary tool of cognition. If *he feels* that it is permissible to rob, assault, and/or murder innocent victims, then this is the only evidence he needs to certify such a belief. Rational moral principles are anathema to him. The only "thinking" he does, i.e., expenditure of mental energy, is to concoct scams to help him "get away" with his crimes.

Rational thinking—meaning the employment of mind power to gain knowledge and then apply it to such positive, life-promoting activities as productive business, technology, science, philosophy, the arts, education, etc.—is alien and not a part of his existence.

His view of reality is necessarily social, i.e., focused on other people. He does not perform honest work, which means that he does not deal with nature in a productive attempt to grow food, build houses, cure diseases, etc. Therefore, his only chance to survive is as a parasite off of the productive work of others. His attitude, in effect, is: "others produce, I steal from the producers." People— his victims and prospective victims—are his sole reality. Are there immutable laws of nature, including of human nature, with which his criminal activities irrevocably clash? Alternatively, is there a God whose will governs the universe, and who has commanded a different manner of life? At the explicit, intellectual level, he is not interested in such questions; at the implicit, emotional level, his answers are: "no."

His view of human beings is that they are impulse-riddled, desire-driven creatures in violent conflict with others for the spoils of human existence. Men are predatory creatures—in effect, great white sharks with a sophisticated brain—and one must fight to the death to grab whatever gratifies one's urges. The English philosopher, John Stuart Mill, once remarked that it is better to be a discontented Socrates than a contented pig; meaning, of course, that man's rational faculty, especially his commitment to moral principles, elevates him— even if temporarily unhappy—far above the level of mere brute animals. But a thug's philosophy necessarily reverses this assessment: it is superior to be an animal momentarily content from a surfeit of eating, belching, and scratching than to be a rational, morally principled human being.

The gangster's view of ethics is, therefore, brutally simple: it is permissible to criminally indulge one's desires and avoid getting caught—to impose one's will on others—and to victimize innocent people on whatever scale one can get away with. On his view, it is not that a thug is morally wrong—and the police, seeking to curtail his criminal activities, are morally right. Rather, it is that they are different—they struggle—and the stronger (or more cunning) side prevails. Principles of right and wrong are not part of a gangster's philosophy; these are replaced by considerations of strength and weakness.

Politically, he has contempt for law and the criminal justice system that protects the innocent from his vicious depredations. To him, anarchy—a lawless non-system of gang violence and mob rule—is preferable to civilized human society.

These examples serve to illustrate a principle: The major questions of philosophy are of the greatest importance to man's life. Every individual, in order to live, must hold some answer to three central questions: "What kind of universe is it?" "How do I know?" "What should I do?" Observe that even the brutes among the human race that eschew productive effort and choose to seek survival by means of criminal violence, are not immune to a need for philosophy. Even their lives necessarily embody answers to these fundamental questions, however irrational and destructive such answers are.

(Indeed, Adolf Hitler and his Nazi followers, for example, murdered millions of innocent victims based on their philosophy. How did they know of their racial superiority? By means of their "blood and bowels," i.e., their gut-level feelings told them so. What kind of world did they inhabit? One featuring a ceaseless struggle between a "master race" and the inferior races denying and obstructing its rightful dominance. What was the right thing to do? To conquer, enslave, and/or exterminate any of the "inferior peoples" who impeded their plan for global mastery.)

The point is not that philosophy is a mere matter of opinion. The fact that people often disagree regarding life's fundamental questions does not mean that the irrational answers given by men such as Capone or Hitler are philosophically or morally equal to the rational ones provided by men such as Edison. This book will show Ayn Rand's emphatic arguments that philosophy is not a matter of opinion; that philosophy is a science of rational, objectively demonstrable principles. *Rather, the point is that no man—whether rational or irrational, honest or dishonest, life promoting or life destroying—can escape the need of philosophical guidance.*

These three questions form the essence of philosophy's major branches. Metaphysics is the branch of philosophy that answers questions regarding the fundamental nature of reality. Epistemology is the branch that answers questions regarding our means of knowledge. Ethics or morality is the branch that answers questions regarding the right and wrong ways to conduct our lives. These are not the only questions or branches of philosophy, but they are its most fundamental ones, and will come up over and again throughout this book.

Ayn Rand describes these branches of philosophy clearly. Metaphysics, she explains, would not tell a man whether he was in New York City or in Zanzibar. But here is some of what it would tell him: "Are the things you see around you real—or are they only an illusion? Do they exist independent of any observer— or are they created by the observer? Are they the object or the subject of man's consciousness? Are they *what they are* – or can they be changed by a mere act of your consciousness, such as a wish?"[3]

Similarly, epistemology alone will not give man knowledge of biology, morality or accounting (or anything else), but it will give him the means of knowing whether a conclusion has been *proven* true. Epistemology answers such questions as: "Does man acquire knowledge by a process of reason—or by sudden revelation from a supernatural power? Is reason a faculty that identifies and integrates the material provided by man's senses—or is it fed by innate ideas, implanted in man's mind before he was born? Is reason competent to perceive reality—or does man possess some other cognitive faculty which is superior to reason [such as feeling, revelation or 'a woman's intuition?'] Can man achieve certainty—or is he doomed to perpetual doubt?"[4]

Ethics, the third of philosophy's fundamental branches, depends on the first two. It deals with the critical questions of right and wrong; with what men should do, and what they should not. But it is impossible for man to know what he should and should not do until he knows the nature of the universe, the nature of his means of cognition, and his own nature. On the basis of his answers to the questions of metaphysics and epistemology, he will answer the questions of ethics: "What is good or evil for man—and why? Should man's primary concern be a quest for joy—or an escape from suffering? Should man hold self-fulfillment—or self-destruction—as the goal of his life? Should man pursue his values—or should he place the interest of others above his own? Should man seek happiness—or self-sacrifice?"[5]

The specific answers an individual gives to these questions shape the course of his life. For example, an individual, such as Thomas Edison, who is committed to reason, a lawful universe, and a man's right to honestly pursue his own loves, logically devotes himself to productive work (in his case, specifically in the field of scientific research) and his own personal achievements and happiness. A different individual, such as Al Capone, who is convinced that desires—not reason—are his means of gaining knowledge, that the world is a brutal struggle over the spoils of ceaseless conflict, and that it is morally permissible to victimize other men to whatever extent he can get away with, logically devolves into an existence of violent crime.

Philosophy, Ayn Rand holds, is the science that rules man's life on earth. Two sub-points make up this truth. One is that philosophy is supremely important, because it asks and answers the most fundamentals questions of human life, questions every man must confront as a condition of living well. The other is that philosophy is inescapable; even those who neither study nor think about it, like the criminal brutes described above, cannot avoid holding views regarding it. We have no choice about holding a philosophy of life. The only choice we have is whether we hold our philosophy explicitly or implicitly, consciously or subconsciously, intellectually or emotionally, in our control or out of it. Those who reject philosophy merely reject thinking about it; they do not realize that they cannot escape holding philosophical views at an emotional level.

Since societies are merely groups of individuals living together in the same geographical areas, they are nothing but the sum total of men's thoughts, values, emotions, and actions. What one observes, therefore, is that just as philosophy governs the life of an individual, so it similarly governs the life of an entire society. Briefly, take the history of the United States of America as an example.

To begin, consider America at its founding period more than 200 years ago. The intellectual climate in which the nation was conceived was the 18th century Enlightenment. Reason was the dominant epistemological principle: men were held to be rational beings, the mind was venerated, science was admired, faith and religious authority were questioned, and freedom—the Rights of Man—was the leading political principle.

Man conceived as a rational being, rather than as a sinful creature permeated by licentious desires, had monumental consequences. It meant that man the individual—man the rationally thinking individual—had self-discipline, moral worth, and an inviolable right to his own life. It followed from this that men could be self-governing, and were not to be commanded by the king, aristocracy, or clergy. Free minds and free men required free political institutions: the rights to life, liberty, property, and the pursuit of happiness; similarly, they required the right to freedom of intellectual expression—of speech and of writing—to freedom of religion, and to freedom to vote their own consciences. An individual's life no longer belonged to the tribe, the king, the emperor, the state, the Church, or God; it now belonged to himself.

In the 19th century, a capitalist economic system developed logically from these basic principles. If a man has a right to his own mind, his own body, his own life, then he has a right to the goods produced by his mental and bodily effort: he has a right to property. Similarly, if he has a right to pursue happiness, then, as an integral part of it, he has a right to work honestly and strenuously in pursuit of economic prosperity. He has a right to pursue profit and to retain what he earns. On the basis of individual rights and capitalism, America of that period was the politically freest and economically wealthiest nation that had yet existed.

To some degree, those same moral and philosophical principles still animate America of the 21st century, but, at the same time, they have been significantly diluted by contrasting ideas that in the past 100 years have become prevalent in the country. Increasingly, the moral ideal that a man must sacrifice for society has become dominant in America. Morally, it is held that individuals must provide selfless service to the poor, the elderly, the sick—to society as a whole. Epistemologically, commitment to rationality—to a tough-minded fact orientation—has been largely supplanted by a "compassionate" emotionalism, including an alleged sympathy for the needy.

There certainly remains the idea that an individual should seek his own profit, success, and happiness—but it is modulated now, combined into a mixed moral view that freedom and individual rights entail social obligations. Politically, this mixed morality has led to a mixed economy. The country is no longer an individualistic bastion of near-laissez-faire capitalism; it is now a mixed economy welfare state, combining individual rights with social duties, freedom with government controls, private property with social welfare programs, capitalism with socialism, etc.

To cite several examples: both religion and contemporary secularism generally denigrate reason—the religionists in favor of faith, the modernists in support of emotionalism, i.e., the belief that a man's feelings or emotions provide him with understanding of life's fundamental truths. Politically, conservatives and liberals promote anti-intellectual authoritarianism: one side calls for uncritical obedience to God, and the other to the state. It follows from these antecedent principles that Republicans and Democrats alike support a morality of self-sacrifice—Republicans as a patriotic duty to the nation, Democrats as moral obligation to the poor.

With such principles increasingly dominant, the country's gradual creep towards political statism has been logically inevitable. Whether the politicians seek to ban abortion rights, prohibit the teaching of evolution, censor the Internet, expand the FCC's authority to control radio and television, increase governmental power of eminent domain, impose environmental restrictions on the drilling of oil or the construction of nuclear plants, establish such "alphabet agencies" as the SEC, the FDA, OSHA (or a dozen others) to control productive

businessmen, force working people to carry on their backs non-productive welfare recipients, or a hundred comparable violations—the principle remains the
same: the rights of honest Americans to guide their lives by their own rational
thinking—in pursuit of their own happiness—are being curtailed. reduced

The differences in America's political past and present are grounded in contrasting answers to philosophical questions: Are men fundamentally rational or
primarily emotional beings? Should they pursue their own happiness or sacrifice
themselves for others? Do they possess an inalienable right to their own lives or
do their lives belong to the state? Is freedom or government control, capitalism
or socialism, the ideal political-economic system? Is it possible to effectively
combine these contrasting theories into a work-able whole, i.e., can the emerg-
ing contradictory claims be resolved? If so, by reference to what principle(s)? If
not, what should men do then?

The specific answers a society gives to the fundamental questions of philosophy shape the course of its existence.

"Philosophy studies the *fundamental* nature of existence, of man, and of
man's relationship to existence." Or, to state the point alternatively: "Philosophy…is the fundamental force shaping every man and culture. It is the science
that guides men's [rational] faculty, and thus every field of endeavor that counts
on this faculty. The deepest issues of philosophy are the deepest root of men's
thought…their action…their history—and, therefore, of their triumphs, their
disasters, their future."[6]

Philosophy rules man's life at both the individual and the social level. This
is what makes the field of such importance, and the deepest reason we must
study it: *to rationally understand and choose the fundamental ideas that will
guide our lives, and not to be uncritically controlled by the philosophy held by
others.*

"You have no choice about the necessity to integrate your observations,
your experiences, your knowledge into abstract ideas, i.e., into principles. Your
only choice is whether these principles are true or false, whether they represent
your conscious, rational convictions – or a grab-bag of notions snatched at random…"[7]

What does Ayn Rand have to say on these critical questions of human life?
What does the philosophy of Objectivism tell us regarding existence, man,
knowledge, right and wrong, an ideal society? How does her philosophy urge us
to conduct our lives?

Ayn Rand's answers are clear. In terms of the examples presented above:
she supports an uncompromising rationality as opposed to faith or emotionalism.
She upholds a natural universe inherently lawful, as opposed to a malleable
world subordinate to either supernatural decree or men's earthly whim. She
stands for the pursuit of personal happiness and rejects self-sacrifice. She proudly defends individual rights and limited Constitutional government, and repudiates all forms of statism; the political-economic freedom of America's founding
period is, therefore, vastly superior to the mixed economy farrago of today.

What are the arguments supporting such claims? What is Ayn Rand's case
for their truth? These are the questions the rest of this book will answer.

Chapter 2

Values as the Meaning of Life

Readers of Ayn Rand's novels generally notice how purposeful, proud, and fulfilled her heroes are. These readers often raise the question: How realistic is it for her men and women to be so happy in a world torn by moral and psychological conflict? For example, in the current day, anti-heroes dominate serious literature and film; leading public figures are often guilty of crimes and/or serious moral transgressions; and some men's lives are fraught with psychological problems, including struggles with alcohol and drugs. And yet, in *The Fountainhead* Howard Roark proceeded purposefully and serenely forward, overcoming daunting obstacles, reaching his goals, gaining everything he desired. Readers wonder: Is this possible in real life? Are human beings capable of achieving such exalted moral stature? Can one live in the same manner as an Ayn Rand hero?

To answer this question, let's consider several passages from her novels, scenes that dramatize the ennobled stature of Ayn Rand's heroes, and then proceed to extract from them some explanatory principles. In savoring and analyzing her heroes, it is helpful to remember this: she often pointed out that she became a philosopher as a necessary means of understanding the deeper principles animating her characters.

In the first passage, the hero of *The Fountainhead*, the uncompromising architect, Howard Roark, witnesses the opening of his innovative apartment complex, the Enright House. Roark, who earlier had to close his office and work in a granite quarry because of lack of support for his revolutionary designs, savors his triumph. Hatless, standing at a parapet overlooking the East River in New York City, head thrown back and face uplifted toward the sun, he experiences the joyous pride of his accomplishment. A photographer, there to cover the opening for a local paper, sees Roark.

The newsman thinks of something that has long puzzled him: "he had always wondered why the sensations one felt in dreams were so much more intense than anything one could experience in waking reality—why the horror was

11

so total and the ecstasy so complete—and what was the extra quality which could never be recaptured afterward; the quality of what he felt when he walked down a path through tangled green leaves in a dream, in an air full of expectation, of causeless, utter rapture—and when he awakened he could not explain it, it had been just a path through some woods." The photographer thinks of it now because, for the first time, he sees that additional quality in a waking moment—sees it in Roark's face uplifted toward his building.[1]

One more scene will provide sufficient information to draw an important conclusion. As Roark's new ideas gradually caught hold, he worked on three major projects simultaneously: the Cord Building—an office tower in midtown Manhattan; the Aquitania Hotel on Central Park South; and the Stoddard Temple—a shrine to the human spirit—far to the north on the bluffs overlooking the Hudson River. His lover, Dominique Francon, posed for the statue for his temple.

Roark arrived one night at the Temple's construction site to find the sculptor, Steven Mallory, and Dominique working late. Mallory, who knew nothing of Roark's relationship with Dominique, told the architect that they were not doing well, that Dominique could not quite capture the quality he sought. Dominique got dressed but took no part in the conversation. She stood and gazed at Roark. Suddenly, she threw off her robe and posed naked again. Then Mallory saw what he had struggled to see all day. "He saw her body standing before him straight and tense, her head thrown back...but now her body was alive, so still that it seemed to tremble, saying what he had wanted to hear: a proud, reverent, enraptured surrender to a vision of her own..."[2]

There are numerous similar scenes in *The Fountainhead* and *Atlas Shrugged*. What they show is that the essence of Ayn Rand's heroes is to burn with passion for values. Howard Roark is ecstatic at the completion of his building. Dominique experiences such reverence for Roark's achievements and character that the mere sight of him fills her with inspiration. In *Atlas Shrugged*, Dagny Taggart's love for her railroad, and Hank Rearden's for both his steel mills and Dagny herself, illustrate an identical theme. These men and women create deep meaning in their lives, which are then filled with joyous excitement. Further, they recognize that value achievement is a means to an end—their life and happiness. They understand that in order to live well, to flourish, to experience joy and exultation, they must pursue values that will, in fact, lead to these outcomes. In subsequent chapters, we will explore the specific values Ayn Rand held every individual should pursue, the means by which he should pursue them, and the reason such values are objective, i.e., derived fundamentally from facts, from reality, and not from subjective whim. But here, the preliminary point is that a rational man sees something as a value because he understands it improves his wellbeing—it contributes to both the sustenance and the enjoyment of his time on earth. Architecture, for example, is both the means by which Roark productively supports his life—and the most fundamental source of meaning in it.

Therefore, the initial questions to be discussed are: What does it mean to actually value something? And, related: What role do personal values play in promoting an individual's happiness?

To these questions Ayn Rand's answer is that values are those things or persons that fill a man's life with significance and purpose, those things that he considers worthy, valuable, important, the things he is willing to work for—to get or to keep. In Ayn Rand's words: "'Value' is that which one acts to gain and/or keep." Perhaps the key term in that definition is "acts." Values are always the object of an action. Whether a man loves education or money or art or a beautiful home or a particular man or woman or children or any and all of the above, his values are those things he considers so important that they impel him to purposeful, goal-directed action. In this regard, values must be carefully distinguished from dreams, wishes, and fantasies.[3]

For example, if a man states that five million dollars would be an enormous benefit to his life, but takes no practical steps to earn it, the money cannot properly be said to be one of his values; rather, it is no more than a wish or a pleasant fantasy. What it would take to transform this dream into a value would be action. If the individual gets a job and starts to earn money; if he works out a budget and begins to save; if he accepts a second job and saves all of the money he earns from it; if he invests his money and carefully monitors his gains; if he does all of this, then it can truthfully be claimed that wealth is a value to this man.

An old saying states that actions speak louder than words, and nowhere is this as true as in the realm of values. Every man can identify his actual values—and those of others—by identifying what each individual pursues in action.

Ayn Rand's theory is one that proudly upholds personal values and a life filled with the things and persons an individual loves. For example, an individual might esteem an education in computer science, or a career in teaching, or a love relationship with a particular man or woman, or starting a family and rearing children, or one of a hundred other life-affirming goals. Whatever positive values an individual holds, he should indefatigably pursue them. Human beings, Ayn Rand argues, should seek their own happiness. They are not obligated to serve the needs of their family, to offer selfless service to God, or to sacrifice themselves for society. They should not renounce personal values. Rather, they should live and act selfishly.

To be self-ish, in Ayn Rand's theory, is to hold and pursue meaningful, life-enhancing values. If a man were to be truly unselfish, and actually attempt to practice a self-sacrifice code, then he would have to renounce his personal values; the more urgent the value(s) he surrendered, the more "noble" his sacrifice would be considered. So, for example, if a young man surrenders the woman he loves to satisfy his mother's expectations, by these standards he is virtuous; if he additionally relinquishes career aspirations, his own apartment, and an independent life to stay home and care for her, the conventional code deems him even more "saintly." But after sacrificing his love, his career, and his autonomy, his life will be empty, drained of personal meaning, filled with only resentment and bitterness.

In *The Fountainhead*, the story of Catherine Halsey provides a perfect example—and a cautionary tale. After she surrenders every personal value—her education, her prospective marriage, her ambition—to serve her uncle, Ellsworth Toohey, and join his "humanitarian" cause, she subsists in a hollow state, an empty, bitter husk, which had once contained a vibrantly innocent soul. The selfless surrender of one's values logically necessitates the draining of all that provides meaning in one's life—and the miserably unfulfilled existence that inexorably follows.

Selfishness, properly understood, involves a commitment to one's self. The deeper question, therefore, becomes: What, fundamentally, is a man's self? Ayn Rand's answer is: at one level, his values, the things he considers most impor- tant; at a deeper level, his mind – the thinking he performed in identifying and choosing those values. There is a scene in *The Fountainhead* that perfectly illus- trates Ayn Rand's theory of selfishness as adherence to one's own values and mind.

Roark at first struggles because his method of designing is radically new. Near the end of Part One, he has had no commissions for months, he is down to a few dollars in his bank account, and he is overdue on his payment of rent and utilities. His hopes are pinned on the prospective commission to design the Manhattan Bank Building. The Board of Directors has kept him waiting as they debated their choice. Finally, they offer to hire him—but with one qualification: they demand to make extraneous and inappropriate changes to his design. Though Roark explains that, like a man, a building should have integrity and, similarly, be consistent throughout, the board insists on its alterations in accor- dance with conventional standards. Roark is forced to choose: an important commission, albeit with an adulterated design—or the maintenance of his artis- tic integrity, with a consequent loss of a significant commercial prospect. Roark refuses the commission on those terms, thereby losing the opportunity.

When one of the Board members accuses his uncompromising stand of be- ing "fanatical and selfless," Roark is incredulous.

> "Roark smiled. He looked down at his drawings. His elbow moved a little, pressing them to his body. He said:
>
> 'That was the most selfish thing you've ever seen a man do.'"[4]

Since Roark had just rejected a major commission in the heart of New York City, which would have brought him money, fame, and increased opportunities in order to stand by a moral principle – the preservation of his building's integ- rity – the discerning reader of *The Fountainhead* will ask: How is this selfish? What is selfish about Roark's action? The answer to these questions penetrates to the heart of Ayn Rand's revolutionary moral theory.

We have already seen that, on Ayn Rand's understanding, selfishness in- volves commitment to one's self. If the essence of one's self is one's values and the judgment employed in choosing those values, then the question becomes: what is Roark's self? In *The Fountainhead*, Roark's value hierarchy is made abundantly clear: architecture of his kind— "My work done my way" —stands at the top of his personal pantheon. It is instructive to note his answer to Henry Cameron regarding his reasons for his commitment to his kind of architecture.

He states: "Because I love this earth. That's all I love. I don't like the shape of things on this earth. I want to change them." "For whom?" [Cameron asks.] "For myself." Roark seeks to transform this earth, to make its structures beautifully functional, to implement an architectural vision that he alone can see—one recognizable to others only through the actualization of his genius. This is the animating purpose of his life. Additionally, of course, there exist several persons who are also of great importance to him, notably Dominique Francon, Gail Wynand, and Henry Cameron. These are Roark's highest values.[5]

Money, although a value, is of lesser importance to him. He wants to make money; like any honest man, he knows he must support himself by his own work; and he expects to be paid—as a rule, he does not give his designs away for nothing. But he wants to get paid for designing *his* kind of building. Roark seeks to build a successful *long-term* practice—with its attendant prosperity— and recognizes that the only effectual means to such an end is to offer his clients works of matchless integrity. He understands that wealth earned in this manner is a superlative good; but that money will provide him no benefit if, in the exchange, he gives up his mind, judgment, and soul, i.e., the very things that make his life and work so precious to him.

Similarly, recognition—when it comes from individuals like Dominique or Austen Heller, who understand and admire his work for the right reasons—is a value. But the right reasons include preeminently the recognition of the design's flawless consistency, which is not to be breached. A related general point is that a rational man chooses to enter into human relationships, business or personal, only because the values shared with others enable such relationships to enhance his wellbeing: they bring educational progress, commercial opportunities, and/or the joy of intimacy, friendship or love. Roark's relationships—with Cameron, Dominique, Wynand, et. al.—are on the basis of shared values and, consequently, bring great meaning into his life.

In brief, Roark remains true to that which is primary to his life and happiness, and refuses to betray it for what are—to him—secondary benefits.

(It should be noted as an important derivative point that there is full congruence between selfishness in Ayn Rand's sense and benevolent goodwill toward one's fellow man. It is eminently possible—indeed, normal— that as one benefits one's self, others benefit, as well. Properly understood, another person's attainment of values is no threat to one's own achievements, and one's own achievements are no threat to anyone else's. To the contrary, in pursuing his own interest, a rational man in the process often helps others advance their selfish interests. For example: by aiding those he loves—his friends, family members, wife, children, et. al.—a rational man advances both their happiness and his own. If he loves his career, whether as teacher, physician, businessman, etc., and works to the conscientious best of his ability, he simultaneously earns his living, takes pride and fulfillment in his work, and benefits all those who have the opportunity to interact with him: his students, patients, customers, et. al. More broadly, if he recognizes that honest men are an enormous benefit to his life—and he to theirs—then his relationships of trading values for values will be fulfilling to all involved. There is, Ayn Rand argued, no clash of interests between truly rational, selfish individuals.)[6]

It is eminently possible to benefit both oneself and others. But it is logically impossible to both fulfill and sacrifice oneself, to both pursue and surrender important values, to gain happiness and selflessly relinquish the personal values upon which happiness depends.

To be true to the self is to be true to one's values. This is exactly what Roark does. He remains true to his highest value, refusing to sacrifice it. To sacrifice is to give up a higher value for a lesser value or a non-value. It is not a sacrifice if a man gives up something of little or no importance to him, in order to gain something more valuable. *For Roark, it would be a sacrifice to adulterate his design in order to obtain money and fame.* That would be surrendering his highest value for things of lesser or no importance. This he refuses to do.

Roark's striking words to the Board regarding his selfishness express his commitment to remain true to his values, to the essence of his self, in action and though under severe financial duress. In this scene, Ayn Rand, in effect, dramatizes the meaning of Polonius's famous words to Laertes in *Hamlet*: "To thine own self be true." For when a man is true, in action, to his supreme values, it is his self that he honors above all. This is selfishness in Ayn Rand's sense of the term.

In real life, a loving parent will save money for his child's education, possibly forgoing a new car or some other luxury. A young married couple, living in their first apartment, might scrimp on vacations or recreation in order to gain the money necessary for a down payment on a house of their own. A serious college student will study for long hours and possibly hold a job, thereby curtailing elements of his social life, because he is working toward a future career of great significance to him. All of these persons and thousands more, are true to their values. None of them are willing to undermine or betray that which is of utmost importance to them. All of them are, in Ayn Rand's sense, properly selfish.

Further, notice the practicality of Roark's selfish commitment to his principles. He knows that sacrificing the integrity of his design will make him miserable, not happy. Additionally, it is true that the Manhattan Bank Building will establish his reputation—but as what? As a man willing to compromise his designs. The Board's version of his building *will* attract clients to him, but ones that prefer the debased in art to the flawlessly consistent. His type of clients, the ones who admire only the best in men and their work—the Austen Hellers, Roger Enrights, Gail Wynands—will be repulsed by a building that has sold its soul. It would take Roark years to live down that building. He recognizes that only consistent selfishness—a scrupulous commitment to his values, an inviolate integrity—will enable him to reach the practical success to which he aspires. People often mistakenly equate "practicality" with gaining as much wealth as possible. Certainly, Ayn Rand holds that wealth well earned is a great value. In reality, practicality includes earning wealth, but is a broader concept. It means attaining your personal values and gaining fulfillment and happiness. Roark is a superbly practical man, because, by remaining unswervingly true to his values, he brings them to an exultant fruition. *triumphant accomplishment*

Roark's actions in this scene illustrate an important principle of the Objectivist ethics: the equivalence of the moral and the practical. It is only by doing what is morally proper that Roark is able to achieve practical success, i.e., only by preserving the integrity of his design can he fulfill his aspirations on his own terms, and therefore be happy. On the other hand, had Roark violated his principles by permitting the Board to compromise his design, any commercial "success" he would have thereby gained would be meaningless. Devoid of the pride that comes only from his work done his way, his life would be empty and painful, not joyously fulfilled. Contrary to popular belief, it is not necessary to sell one's soul for practical success. *Indeed, it is not possible.* Morality and practicality, in fact, stand in direct—not inverse—proportion to each other. (In subsequent chapters, we will examine the deeper reasons for this. We will come to see that, to Ayn Rand, being moral means enacting an unbreached commitment to rationality—the exact method required to achieve one's values in practice and thereby gain happiness.)

The selfish man is one who meets two criteria: 1. he holds principles and forms values that will, in fact, lead to his long-term wellbeing—he is not self-destructive; and 2. he remains consistently true to his life-promoting ideas in practice. This—nothing else and nothing less—is loyalty to the self. The selfless man is one who either never does such thinking to form personal values—or who betrays the ideals, convictions, and commitments he does hold. Such a person is selfless in a literal sense—he lacks a self, i.e., in some form he surrenders the independent judgment, the rational thinking, that enables men to form actual values. In some manner, he then permits his life to be dominated by others.

The technical name in moral philosophy for Ayn Rand's theory is: *egoism.* Egoism is the moral theory stating that an individual should be the beneficiary of his own actions. It endorses self-interest, the pursuit of one's own happiness. In its polemical aspect, it cautions each man against the sacrifice of his self, of the goals and values most precious to him. It emphasizes the solemn necessity of each individual to pursue his own life and personal happiness.

In order to understand how revolutionary a philosophy Objectivism is, it is necessary to distinguish its theory of egoism from the two contrasting theories prevalent in modern Western society. The first such theory, *selflessness* (the code of *self-sacrifice*) will be examined here; the other, *cynical exploitativeness,* in the subsequent chapter.

Selflessness is any moral code that exhorts a man to place something—be it God, other people, the state, etc.—above his own self. *Altruism*—the doctrine that a man must sacrifice himself specifically for other people—is one dominant version of the ethics of selflessness. But Ayn Rand's egoist ethics unconditionally repudiates selflessness in any and all of its manifestations, regardless of the purported beneficiary.

Ayn Rand's repudiation of any self-sacrificial moral code is based on her revolutionary identification that a man's self is his mind, his thinking, the judgment he deploys to choose his personal values. If he sacrifices his values for any reason, then he necessarily sacrifices his mind to whoever promulgates those reasons. In expunging the effect—his values—he effaces their cause—his thinking. So, to revert to a previous example: if a man loves a woman and chooses her to be his wife, but renounces his desire to satisfy his family, he abjures more than his love relationship; he betrays his soul, his consciousness, his mind—his judgment by means of which he chose her. The value judgments—and hence, the beliefs—of other people then necessarily control his life.

In *The Fountainhead*, Peter Keating perfectly exemplifies this lamentable principle. Early in life, he does occasionally think and value independently. In his youth, for instance, he cherishes painting; as a young man, he loves Catherine Halsey—but he yields both of these budding passions to satisfy his mother, Ellsworth Toohey, and society more broadly. It is his own mind Keating thereby treats as expendable or inconsequential—a faculty that can be discarded in favor of uncritical obedience. It is his very survival instrument (as we will study in detail in subsequent chapters) that Keating or any other forlorn conformist treats as dispensable jetsam. goods cast overboard to lighten up ship

Similarly, in real life, a politician who compromises his principles because they are not popular with the voters—or a businessman who sells a product that, in his judgment, is debased, because it is craved by the consumers—or a high school student who surrenders clean living because his "friends" are drug users—or any one of countless other examples—has betrayed more than his specific values. To the extent that he sacrifices those ideals or goals dearest to him, to that extent he has repudiated his mind; to that extent, he will then be a mindless drone, unquestioningly following the judgment of others, who are thereby granted omnipotence in his life.

In light of such a deplorable truth, it must be understood that, according to the code urging selflessness, the greater the value surrendered, the more "noble" the sacrifice. (It is not a sacrifice to relinquish something that one values only marginally—or not at all.) But a man's mind is more fundamental than his highest value; it is that *by means of which* he values, that which makes valuing and thereby life possible. To surrender it is to surrender the very possibility of valuing. The appalling truth regarding the moral code of self-sacrifice is that it constitutes unremitting war on a man's mind.

> "It is your *mind* that they want you to surrender—all those who preach the creed of sacrifice, whatever their tags or their motives...Those who start by saying: "It is selfish to pursue your own wishes, you must sacrifice them to the wishes of others"—end up by saying: "It is selfish to uphold your convictions, you must sacrifice them to the convictions of others.
>
> This much is true: the most *selfish* of all things is the independent mind that recognizes...no value higher than its judgment of truth."[7]

Altruism does not merely demand the surrender of values—that which brings meaning to a man's life—but worse: it requires the surrender of the mind, the source of his values. By analogy, altruism does not merely dig up flourishing plants by their roots; it poisons the soil in which they grow, rendering impossible the flowering of robust life.

There are two main points in this chapter, each with its contrasting negative: one is that personal values provide the meaning of life—and that to surrender them is to empty life of all meaning. The second is that the source of a man's values is his independent thinking—and that to sacrifice his values is to thereby surrender his mind.

But Ayn Rand's theory of egoism repudiates more than merely altruism. It also differs sharply from the code that has conventionally been contrasted with all forms of self-sacrifice; the theory that claims it is morally permissible for a man—in pursuit of his own interest—to victimize others; that the attempt to attain personal happiness involves and justifies the sacrifice of others to self; that selfishness, in short, entails the exploitation of other people. Let us now turn to that view.

Chapter 3

Egoism vs. Cynical Exploitativeness

Ayn Rand's theory of egoism stands in dramatic opposition to the code that can best be described as *cynical exploitativeness*, the theory that human life is indistinguishable from a jungle struggle, that others are a man's natural prey who exist solely for him to use and victimize. This is the code of the liar, the cheat, the criminal, of any man who seeks gain by duplicitous, dishonest methods. The exploiter is not interested in *working* for, i.e., *earning* what he wants; he doesn't seek to *create* values but to *appropriate* them from others.

Where the self-sacrifice code eschews self-interest, the code of cynical exploitativeness utterly misconceives it. Ayn Rand repudiates the exploitative theory not because it is selfish (in fact, it is not), but because its view of man is thoroughly irrational.

According to Ayn Rand's conception of egoism, each man bears responsibility for his own life. He must gain the values his life requires—and.he must do so by his own effort. Egoism, in other words, is a principle permitting no double standards. Each man must work hard and *earn* his values and his happiness, not seek them by victimizing innocent others. Each person makes his own way in life—and none may adopt the attitude: others produce while I consume. Egoism permits no seeking of the unearned. Just as an individual is not obligated to sacrifice for others, so they are not duty-bound to serve him. In short, the same principle that sanctions one individual's pursuit of values sanctions the value pursuit of every other individual.

This point is succinctly summarized in the oath sworn by the hero of *Atlas Shrugged:* "I swear by my life and my love of it that I will never live for the sake of another man, nor ask another man to live for mine." This code advocates a *non-sacrificial* way of life—a mode of conduct that repudiates both altruism and cynical exploitativeness, both the sacrifice of self to others and the sacrifice of others to self.[1] Although, historically, altruism and exploitation have postured as opposites, Ayn Rand pointed out that they differ only as variations on a theme. Neither has outgrown the primitive call for human sacrifice. They differ merely regarding the question of who is to be sacrificed to whom. The altruist claims that self should be sacrificed to others; the cynical exploiter argues that others should be sacrificed to self. But they agree that a non-sacrificial mode of life is impossible. The two codes, taken together, constitute a "cannibal morality" necessitating that some men get eaten by others.[2]

But in fact, human beings are not predatory creatures inhabiting a "dog-eat-dog" world; they are rational beings who survive and prosper only by creating the values their lives require, not by plundering them from conquered or swindled victims.

In both *The Fountainhead* and *Atlas Shrugged*, Ayn Rand dramatizes the point that men survive by productivity, not by parasitism. The goods and services our lives require must be created by men's effort. Human beings must think and work. The houses, for example, must be built. The medicines must be researched and developed. The food must be grown—and much more. These creative processes require rational effort by men. Liars, cheats, grafters, criminals, dictators, and conquerors contribute nothing to human productivity. That some might steal or plunder wealth in the short term does not alter the basic fact that man's values must be *created*. Human beings survive and prosper by means of *achievement, not theft*. Productive men can carry on their backs a certain number of parasites, but if the preponderance of people attempted survival by such dishonest means, human society would collapse. *It is in a man's self-interest to produce and achieve, not to seek values by duplicitous and parasitical means*.

"There is a fundamental moral difference between a man who sees his self-interest in production and a man who sees it in robbery." One difference between such men lies in the social consequences of their actions—for both themselves and others. The robber victimizes others while the producer benefits himself and, as a consequence, others as well. In the long run (and in a free society) the thief is caught and incarcerated while the producer prospers. The exploiter seeks to live out a contradiction—in effect, a double standard: human beings must produce in order to survive and prosper, but I don't have to. In pursuing this contradiction, he makes enemies of rational, productive men, and necessarily surrounds himself with fellow scoundrels, the only type of men willing to consort with such as him. He consequently spends his life sneaking, hiding, concealing the truth, living a covert, subterranean existence, a desperate man, on the run from the law and from society's most honest members. This is a prescription for failure and misery. By contrast, honest men, precisely because they consistently uphold the principle that man must produce to survive, lead an opposite kind of life—one of openness, of pride, and of an utter lack of skeletons hidden in their closets. They can, in the immortal words of Dominique Francon in *The Fountainhead*, "stand naked in full sunlight."[3]

The more fundamental point, however, regards a man's relationship to nature, not to society. Human beings do not live in a Garden of Eden in which all the goods their survival requires exist readymade for the taking. It is not society that prohibits man's life as a parasitical non-producer; it is nature. Reality requires man to produce if he is to flourish: the productive person lives in accordance with this fact of nature, but the parasite fights it. It is a battle no man can win. Society will imprison him—but nature will cause him to starve when he runs out of victims.

In the climactic scene of *The Fountainhead*, Howard Roark points out that human beings have but two possibilities in their quest for survival: they can either face nature independently, learning to create values—or they can seek survival parasitically, through the intermediary of the independent men. "The creator's concern is the conquest of nature. The parasite's concern is the conquest of men."[4]

Paraphrasing Ayn Rand: one type seeks to conquer nature; the other to conquer those who conquer nature.

The creators and producers of values can reap a harvest of abundance; they can build, grow, construct, achieve—and prosper. They need no one else. But the parasites choose not to deal with nature—and, therefore, left to their own devices, in the absence of victims, subsist in misery. Viewed in principled terms, therefore, it is clear where an individual's actual self-interest lies.

For example, how much food actually exists today, even in America, the world's wealthiest nation? For what duration of time could that food last? If men chose to end productive work—to cease growing, shipping, and selling food—and to subsist by parasitical means instead, their recourse to robbery and victimization would entail the survival of those most cunning and violent—for all of several additional days. For after the most aggressive brute plundered his final victim of the last morsel on earth, his own process of starvation inexorably ensues.

Considered long-term, as a matter of consistent principle, human well-being requires the creation of values—the *creation* of values, not their plunder. Consequently, a life of honest productivity, and the rejection of parasitism in all of its forms, is the life that Ayn Rand construes as egoistic, and the one she endorses.

The rational case against cynical exploitativeness can be summarized succinctly. The exploitative aspect of such an existence leads an individual to war against society's most honest and productive members, making men's intelligence, their rationality, and their commitment to justice his deadliest foes—and necessarily fills his miserable inner life with fear of being caught, and guilt at the realization that this is all he deserves. Further, the code that urges victimization of others often is combined with the view that *hedonism*—a mindless, indiscriminate pursuit of bodily pleasure—is in a man's self-interest. This aspect of the code generally leads to self-destruction by means of toxic drugs and/or excessive amounts of alcohol. Above all, by repudiating rational productiveness as his mode of survival, he devolves into a hopeless war against human nature—and against reality, which requires productivity of men. Therefore, in every way—socially, psychologically, biologically, and metaphysically—cynical exploitativeness leads only to failure, misery, and, if not quickly corrected, early and unfulfilled death.

Since human beings need to create values in order to survive and flourish, one important question is: How? By what means is a man to gain the values that his life and happiness require? Or, phrased alternatively, according to Ayn Rand the main question of ethics becomes: how does one consistently produce and earn values? This contrasts with what the central question is under both altruism and cynical exploitativeness. To an altruist, the pre-eminent question is: what is the best way to sacrifice my values? To an exploiter, the question is: how am I to survive as an irrational non-producer? Or, in his own terms, the question is: how can I successfully victimize others to gain what I desire?

The anti-egoist schools have simple answers to such questions. The altruist's answer is: all you need is love. By coming to feel compassion or mercy, the able will support the unable, the strong will minister to the weak, the productive will sustain the unproductive and the counter-productive. They hold up as their paradigm example Jesus Christ, on the premise that the real problem is to share the wealth—and that charitable kindness is the solution. How, then, to sacrifice my values? In the way that most benefits society's least productive individuals.

The cynical exploiter responds to the question of how he is to survive as an irrational non-producer with the answer: by victimizing others—by conquering, controlling, manipulating, enslaving or robbing the creators of values. Parasites of every ilk—from common thieves to welfare statists to military conquerors to a plethora of dictators—claim their right to expropriate the wealth created by productive men. How, then, to survive as a helpless non-producer? By deploying whatever weapons one possesses—psychological manipulation, cunning criminal scams, brute physical force, plundering armies, etc.—to trick, bamboozle, con, rob, conquer or enslave the creative, productive men who deal effectually with nature.

Both of the anti-egoist schools proceed from the assumption that the values man's life depends on exist antecedently—and that their "just" distribution is the primary moral question. The exploiter feels he deserves a greater share; and the altruist feels others do. But how did these values come into being? By whose effort and by what means? These are questions the anti-egoists do not care to raise.

But these are questions that Ayn Rand does raise. And because she does, she is able to grasp that it is neither by plunder nor by charity that men survive and prosper on earth—neither by hostility nor by "compassion," neither by brute force nor by "love." For example, the Saddam Husseins of the world produce nothing; they merely grab what others have produced. But the Mother Theresas of the world equally produce nothing; at best, they seek to convince the productive to take care of the non-productive. Which characteristic or faculty actually enables men to produce the values their lives depend on? Ayn Rand's theme in Atlas Shrugged is that reason is that faculty.

The First Statement of the Lesson

Chapter 4

Rationality as the Fundamental Means of Achieving Values

Observe that Ayn Rand's heroes and heroines are men and women of the mind, brilliant thinkers who discover new knowledge or identify innovative methods by which to apply that knowledge to the benefit of man's life. Howard Roark, for example, is an architectural genius; Dagny Taggart, a brilliant businesswoman/engineer; John Galt, a monumental intellect who revolutionizes men's understanding in both physics and philosophy. Are these characters mere fictitious creations on the author's part—or do they have important analogues in reality?

It has been said that we "stand on the shoulders of giants," and the shoulders most responsible for carrying mankind out of the caves and into modern industrial civilization belong to intellectual giants. From Aristotle, who identified the methods of proper reasoning—to Isaac Newton, who revolutionized our understanding of nature—to Thomas Edison, the most accomplished inventor of history—to many other such examples from history—it has been the men of intellectual genius who are fundamentally responsible for mankind's most important advances.

The values human life requires do not exist antecedently in nature; they must be created by human effort. Every one of those values is a creation of the human mind. One life-giving example is the advances in medicine that result in new treatments and cures for lethal diseases. Such medications and surgical methods must be researched and developed, requiring knowledge of the science of biology, which requires the rational mind. Similarly, our houses and buildings require knowledge of architecture, as well as of the principles of engineering and mathematics, which require the mind. Further, the food that mankind grows depends on understanding agricultural science—how to fertilize the soil, how to irrigate, when to rotate crops, when to let the land lie fallow, how to genetically engineer new strains of food, etc. —all of which require the reasoning mind.

Because all values on which human life depend are creations of the rational faculty, Ayn Rand identified the mind as mankind's survival instrument.

All species are endowed by nature with certain characteristics by which they survive. The birds, for example, have wings, which enable them to fly. The lions have claws and fangs, with which to rend their prey. The antelopes have great foot speed, which permits them to outrun the lions. Elephants possess vast size and strength rendering them impervious to predatory attack. These animal species survive by physicalistic attributes and activities. But man lacks the bodily characteristics of these animal species; he is without great size, strength or speed of foot. He possesses no wings, fur, fangs or claws. Nature endows him with one instrument by means of which to seek survival, and only one: reason.

> Man cannot survive except through his mind. He comes on earth unarmed. His brain is his only weapon. Animals obtain food by force. Man has no claws, no fangs, no horns, no great strength of muscle. He must plant his food or hunt it. To plant, he needs a process of thought. To hunt, he needs weapons, and to make weapons – a process of thought.[1]

History abounds with individuals who vividly illustrate Ayn Rand's thesis. One is the great French chemist, Louis Pasteur, whose scientific training and research enabled him to identify microscopic organisms—germs—as the cause of disease; a monumental advance making possible Alexander Fleming's further discovery of penicillin, the so-called "miracle drug," first of the antibiotics.

Similarly, Orville and Wilbur Wright, two bicycle mechanics and self-educated aeronautical engineers, studied for years the principles of aviation, eventually inventing the airplane, leading ultimately to jet engines, international flights, and space travel. In the same era, Thomas Edison invented the electric lighting system, flooding the earth with light and pioneering electricity as a power source.

Earlier, James Watt, the path-breaking Scottish thinker and inventor, diligently studied the properties of steam with the noted chemist, Joseph Black, at the University of Glasgow, gaining insights which he employed to perfect the steam engine. This device enormously augmented the power at man's disposal and made possible the Industrial Revolution's colossal increases in productivity. In each of these cases, and in a thousand more, an individual human mind pioneered breakthroughs that led to immense benefit in men's lives—whether in terms of significantly increased life expectancies, vastly higher living standards, or both.

All such advances underscore the important fact that the knowledge required for human survival and wellbeing must be discovered by man; none of it is innate in his consciousness at birth. Painstakingly, across a span of millennia, great thinkers have identified that a wheel can be created; that crops can be grown; that the sun, not the earth, is the center of our solar system; that the Far East can be reached by sailing west; that germs cause disease; that effective surgery requires antiseptic measures; that medications can be created to kill the harmful germs; that oil can be employed to heat men's homes and power their vehicles; and that electricity can be harnessed to provide brilliant illumination.

Further, such life-enhancing practical achievements are made possible only by prior progress in philosophy and theoretical science that provide men a *rational method* with which to understand the world. For example, Aristotle formulated the rules of proper reasoning, and identified the main errors of reasoning—the fallacies of logic. Galileo recognized that advances in and applications of mathematics were crucial to further men's understanding of physics (and the laws of nature more broadly)—and pioneered the use of quantitative experimentation. Another brilliant scientist, Isaac Newton, laid the foundations for differential and integral calculus, and formulated the universal laws of motion, including his celebrated analysis of gravitation. These great theoretical accomplishments of the mind—and other similar advances—laid the intellectual groundwork making possible the monumental progress described above in such applied fields as medicine and technology, as well as in agricultural science and in other fields.

But Ayn Rand's point has still wider applicability. Men's great achievements in the arts, as well as in the sciences—in the spiritual, as well as in the material realm—are reached by means of brilliant rational thought. Leonardo, Michelangelo, Shakespeare, Goethe, Tolstoy, Beethoven, Chopin, to name merely a few, are neither amateurish dilettantes nor whim-driven emotionalists; rather, they are *geniuses*, i.e., prodigiously profound thinkers. The great artists hold a vision of the world and of man's place in it; they identify significant truths regarding human life; they create vivid artistic means by which to express their insights. As but one example, consider the expansive *understanding*—and of diverse subjects—required by Dostoyevsky to write his masterpiece, *The Brothers Karamazov*, with its complex plot and its penetrating insight into the psychology of evil.

In *Atlas Shrugged*, the brilliant composer, Richard Halley, presents Ayn Rand's theory regarding the source of great art:

> Whether it's a symphony or a coal mine, all work is an act of creating and comes from the same source: from an inviolate capacity to see through one's own eyes—which means: the capacity to perform a rational identification—which means: the capacity to see, to connect and to make what had not been seen, connected and made before. I... know what discipline, what effort, what tension of mind, what unrelenting strain upon one's power of clarity are needed to produce a work of art...[2]

In *The Fountainhead*, Howard Roark sums up this point succinctly: "From this simplest necessity to the highest religious abstraction, from the wheel to the skyscraper, everything we are and everything we have comes from a single attribute of man—the function of his reasoning mind."[3]

Observe the phrase "from the simplest necessity." For rational thinking is also the method by which a family doctor diagnoses and treats an illness—by which a detective pieces together evidence to apprehend a criminal—by which a plumber identifies the source of (and solution to) a troubling leak; and it is the means by which to achieve a plethora of other human values. The principle is: every instance of human beings taking positive, life-promoting actions—from the grandest of scales to the intermediate to the most mundane—involves the application of rationality.

Since reason is the faculty by which human beings create all values—material or spiritual—and since the achievement of values is the means to fulfillment and happiness—it follows that reason is the happiness-creating faculty. It can therefore be propounded, in all solemnity, that reason is "the happy faculty." The point can be stated hypothetically: If human beings seek happiness, then they must maintain, in action, an uncompromising commitment to rationality. To achieve happiness, the effect, men must enact reason, the cause.

Observe the importance of this principle at the personal level, in terms of an individual's own life. For example, an outstanding pupil at school—as a necessary means of achieving excellence—thinks about the material presented: he reads carefully, asks questions, takes notes, prepares conscientiously for exams. Long before graduating high school, he's thinking about college: whether he will enroll—if so, where—what he will study—what he will do upon graduation, etc.

Such an individual does not fall accidentally into a career; he has identified what he values and plans the requisite steps. If he plans to go into law, for example, he researches law schools, investigates options for financing his tuition, thinks about the specific area of law in which he will concentrate, etc. He puts himself on the path toward achieving a life full of values.

To take a different example of the same principle: suppose an individual loves cars and tinkers on them from childhood. He learns facts about automotive mechanics and thinks about a career in the field. Perhaps he attends vocational school to study the subject in depth; almost certainly, he procures a job pumping gas at a local service station and talks to the mechanics in his spare time, gaining knowledge. With experience comes increased responsibility; in time, he's a full-fledged mechanic, applying his learned skills to the repair of countless engines. Eventually, he dreams of opening his own shop—so he works out a budget and saves money; he searches for a suitable location; he learns everything he can from his more experienced colleagues; and eventually, he strikes out on his own—and succeeds.

One important lesson from the above vignette is that "manual labor" in a technologically advanced society is not primarily—much less exclusively—physical; it is predominantly intellectual. An accomplished mechanic diagnoses automotive problems the way a superb physician diagnoses medical ailments; each, to gain expertise, must *understand* his respective field. After all, you could not teach a gorilla to diagnose and repair internal combustion engines. Even if scientists learn to graft an opposable thumb onto the gorilla's hand, so he can grip tools, the gorilla could not do it, because he could not comprehend the nature of the work.

The principle that all human values depend on rational thought can also be established by contrast. For example, another individual, also a student—

although intelligent—is not a thinker. School is more of a social activity for him than a cognitive one, and he neglects his studies. In the short term, he has a few moments of fun—but his enjoyment soon ends under the inexorable weight of failing grades, diminished prospects, and the realization that his struggles are the result of his own lack of effort. Until and unless he chooses to enact more rational policies, he will remain uncertain and unhappy.

Many men and women who were irresponsible carousers in their youth have righted themselves—and they have accomplished this *by the only method of doing so*: by taking a careful re-assessment of their lives. They *think* about what they are doing to themselves; they proceed to *think* about their studies; and then they *think* about their futures. Such conscientious thinking—and only such conscientious thinking—is the path to their greatly improved lives.

Success in education and in all careers, including those involving manual labor, requires thinking, planning, application of the rational mind.

clever   But, an <u>astute</u> individual might ask, what about other important aspects of life? What about friendship, romantic love, parenting? In what manner is reason indispensable in achieving values in these aspects of life, i.e., in fields conventionally regarded as less material, and more emotional or spiritual?

The generally held belief about these important areas of human life is that they are governed by feelings of love, kindness, affection, i.e., by emotions. In fact, these emotions represent a significant aspect of such relationships—but the critical principle remains: all proper human interactions must be governed by reason, not by emotion.

Consider, for example, the different ways in which Howard Roark and Peter Keating approach friendship. Roark befriends Mike Donnigan, Austen Heller, Steve Mallory, Gail Wynand—not Keating or Toohey. He understands that the affection and love he shares with such individuals is crucial but that these emotions are based in his rational recognition of the virtues possessed by such men. He *judges* them to be good men; he *evaluates* their characters as trustworthy; he governs his choices and actions by his mind, not his emotions. As a result, he sustains close friendships with good men over the course of many years. In real life, as in fiction, a rational man seeks out those who are honest, productive, just. He recognizes that other human beings constitute an enormous value, but only if they are men of principle who can be respected and trusted.

By contrast, Peter Keating seeks to indiscriminately befriend everyone. A man lacking moral standards does not value them in others. If others flatter or acclaim or console him, thereby making him *feel* good, he befriends them without regard to their character. It is by such an *emotionalist* method that Keating makes the ruinous error of following the venomous Ellsworth Toohey, thereby committing spiritual suicide. By the end of the story, Keating loses everything, friendship and love, as well as career. Similarly, in real life, irrational men do not hold reality-based, life-promoting values. Since they do not pursue their goals by honest, conscientious effort, they do not esteem or befriend those who do. They surround themselves only with the unprincipled types willing to consort with such as they; and, like Keating, though they may clutter their lives with a multitude of disingenuous "social butterflies," they subsist in miserable loneliness, unable to attain authentic friendship.

A rational man looks at how men conduct themselves in a variety of life's roles: do they strive diligently in school and/or at work? Do they keep their promises? Are they responsible, capably fulfilling all tasks voluntarily undertaken? Are they unswervingly truthful—or guilty of occasional lapses of honesty? Answers to such questions require facts and evidence—and a ruthless commitment to the truth, regardless of one's feelings toward a person. It is possible to have intense positive emotions for a man based on his charm or affability—but an honest man recognizes that more than this is required as the basis of a friendship; he looks not merely for pleasantness of personality but for strength of character. Genuine friendship involves many components, including mutual affection, companionship, good will, etc. But an integral part of the relationship is a rational judgment of another man's trustworthiness, i.e., of his moral character.

This point is of even greater urgency in the field of romantic love. Undeniably, love is an emotion—and a powerful force in human life. But even here, the question must be raised: does reason play a role in a love *relationship*? The answer, in part, is that, yes, precisely because the potential for either joy or heartbreak is so great, an individual must be careful regarding to whom he/she gives his/her heart. This is why rational men and women, even when experiencing powerful initial attraction, characteristically engage in a courtship process. They get to know each other before making love, certainly before entering into a committed relationship, and especially before making the lifetime commitment of marriage.

The phrase "getting to know" each other is an accurate summation of the process. They gain knowledge of the other, as well as of themselves in a romantic relationship; they learn important facts, over time, regarding the other's personality, psychology, and, above all, his/her character. Such *knowledge*, indispensable to a fulfilling love relationship, is gained by means of a cognitive process, and requires a scrupulous application of a man's rational faculty. One proof of this point, although negative, is that many a man and woman have lived to rue the ignoring of cautionary evidence pointing to the failings of the individual he or she desires, above all to the moral failings, i.e., they learn the hard way the result of subordinating facts to feelings. A rational man understands that he must be able to trust his lover with his "heart" and, if necessary, with his life—and, if they choose to have children, with his child's life. The conclusion must be that even when emotions are so strong—indeed, especially then—a man's choices and ensuing actions must be guided by reason.

The same is true of the enormously challenging job of effective parenting. Two critical components of a parent's responsibility are: overseeing the child's cognitive development and providing his moral education. Above all, in a multitude of ways, a competent parent must provide the rational supervision that a child requires. The parent must have knowledge regarding a proper diet, rudimentary medical symptoms and care, requirements of sufficient rest and exercise—and vastly more—as well as knowledge regarding the deeper issues of cognitive and moral education. To love a child is indispensable, but, in itself, insufficient; a loving parent must possess extensive knowledge to rear a child prepared for a successful and fulfilled life. To this end, the most conscientious parents do research regarding child rearing: they read books, talk to their doctor, discuss the important issues with other experienced parents, and, of course, think seriously regarding their child's wellbeing. The knowledge required for effective parenting, as all other knowledge, is a product of man's rational intelligence.

The overall conclusion must be that a fulfilled human life requires a scrupulous, unswerving commitment to reason in every possible context—regarding life-and-death matters, as well as mundane ones; involving human relationships and romance, every bit as much as education and career; in the spiritual aspects of life, as much as in the material ones. Man survives and prospers by the use of his rational mind.

The primary hero of *Atlas Shrugged* makes this point clearly: Every positive action that, in fact, promotes man's earthly life requires the rational mind. A man cannot so much as dig a ditch without knowledge of his goal and the method to attain it.

> Man's life, as required by his nature, is not the life of a mindless brute, of a looting thug or a mooching mystic, but the life of a thinking being—not life by means of force or fraud, but life by means of achievement—not survival at any price, since there's only one price that pays for man's survival: reason.[4]

A fundamental question to be answered, therefore, is: What is distinctive about reason? The answers involve complex philosophical issues, and Ayn Rand's theory can be presented in stages, starting with a simple explanation that can be gradually developed.

Reason is a mental process that requires an uncompromising commitment to facts, to truth, to reality. A rational man permits no other factor to interfere with his grasp of fact—neither his own emotions nor the beliefs of others nor any other consideration.

Practically, an undeviating commitment to reason, to reality, means a relentless devotion to increasing one's knowledge and to upgrading one's skills. Rational men and women understand that their lives and happiness—and that of those they love—depend on knowledge of countless issues and circumstances; they dedicate themselves to attaining exactly that information.

In their education, from first grade through college and, perhaps, beyond, they apply themselves, gaining a deeper understanding of reading, writing, grammar, history, literature, mathematics, science, and more. They know their educations do not terminate with their schooling; for the duration of their lives, they continue to think, to read books, magazines, newspapers, and to seek out intelligent, well-informed individuals as their associates and friends.

Such individuals have active minds and keep apprised of the leading issues of the day, seeking to continuously expand their knowledge of the world they inhabit. Even when the news is unpleasant or frightening, they keep abreast of it, knowing that knowledge is power and that ignorance, far from being a source of bliss or any other positive, is an obstacle in the path of gaining values. Above all, rational individuals are thinkers. They strive to the utmost to understand the events of the world.

Further, successful living requires mastery of practical skills, ranging from such simple tasks as balancing a checkbook to more sophisticated ones like learning use of a computer and the Internet. Indeed, personal computers constitute a good example: some individuals born before the cyber revolution continue to avoid using them—but the most active minds of that generation recognized their great merit and learned to use computers and the Internet to the great enrichment of their lives.

All knowledge and practical skills necessary to advance one's life are a function of rationality. Whether an individual is a genius mastering the cognitive principles necessary to make life-saving breakthroughs in his field—or a first grade teacher striving to clearly apply phonics as the method of teaching reading—or a pizza delivery boy poring over a map, learning the lanes and obscure byways of his town—all of the practical knowledge and skills that improve human life depend on the continual use of the mind.

Ayn Rand points out that the nature of rationality is an unbending allegiance to facts, to truth, to reality—regardless of any countervailing consideration, whether an individual's own feelings, the beliefs of society, or anything else. "Nature, to be commanded, must be obeyed," stated Francis Bacon in a famous aphorism. "Reality, to be successfully lived in, must be acknowledged," could be an aphoristic expression of Ayn Rand's theory.

Whether the facts of a given case are pleasant or unpleasant, benign or malignant, reassuring or frightening, a rational man faces and acknowledges them all; he refuses to evade or deny even painful truths.

An old saying states: "The truth hurts." The claim is erroneously pessimistic. The truth is that *sometimes* the truth immediately hurts, but sometimes a specific set of facts induces happiness when identified, not pain. Either way, the rational individual confronts them all because he knows that this is the only way to consistently place himself on the path to success. His emotional responses to different facts will vary widely, but his willingness to face them universally will remain unwavering.

A fundamental distinction in this regard must be drawn between a long-term and a short-term perspective. In the short run, it might seem tempting to deny an unpleasant fact, on the purported ground that ignorance is bliss. But a rational man recognizes that painful truths do not dissolve or disappear merely because he refuses to acknowledge them. He recognizes that *in the long run* he must, in effect, "take arms against a sea of troubles," if he is to ameliorate a distressing situation. Ignorance is not bliss; in truth, it is merely ignorance—and provides an unmitigated impediment to any successful value quest.   to make better

For example, consider the parent who recognizes that his child is responsible for initiating a fight with a neighbor's child. Although he would prefer his child to be guiltless, the rational parent understands that facts are facts, and that his child's character will not improve unless he recognizes the truth and takes appropriate action. Or: a scientist identifies that the line of research to which he has dedicated years, and from which he expected great results and a possible

Nobel Prize, is actually a dead end. However, his colleagues are still excited about its possibilities, and briefly he is tempted to cover up the data disproving his hypothesis—but, recognizing that falsehoods will not lead to the new vaccine he is striving to create, he presents the full truth and recommences his investigation afresh. Or: a woman discovers evidence that her husband is unfaithful; despite her heartbreak and anger, she investigates, seeking the unvarnished truth, refusing to evade or deny it, knowing that the type of relationship she wants cannot be attained by accepting and living a lie.

Or, to phrase the point in a simple way that a young child can understand: the long-term oral health of regular dental visits provides vastly more value than any supposed short-term benefit gained by evading the necessity of treatment.

To demonstrate the life-and-death importance of an unbreached rationality, consider the following story: a man in his 40s experiences chest pains; scared that this might indicate a heart condition, he refuses to consider the possibility; he tells himself it is only indigestion, and treats it with over-the-counter medication. Though the symptoms persist for months without improvement, he refuses to see a physician. Finally, he suffers a massive heart attack and dies. Such a tragedy is the result of placing other considerations—his fear of having a heart condition, his desire for it to be something innocuous—above and before the facts.

Ayn Rand described such a self-destructive policy as "placing an 'I wish' above an 'it is.'" Its essence is treating one's desires, rather than facts, as the unquestioned primaries of cognition. Since reason is man's survival instrument, any policy of unreason—of denigrating facts, of demoting them, of subordinating them to any consideration whatever—undercuts the use and functioning of man's tool of survival. By what means then are men to survive? Men who choose not to think, to reason, or to honor facts will suffer and die, just as birds would if they could and did choose not to fly. Men, in fact, often choose to be irrational, but they cannot choose irrationality *and* fulfilled, flourishing life; the first negates the second. In any circumstances and under all conditions, the denial of facts is hazardous to a man's physical and mental life.

Irrationality is not ignorance—i.e., it is not an honest error or innocent lack of knowledge. It is *evasion,* the deliberate, willful denial of facts. Whether it's a cocaine user, who pushes aside the knowledge of the damage the drug does to his health—or the Nazis, who ignored every known fact of biology to assert moral superiority based on their blood—or an "economist," who refuses to consider the long-term bankruptcy that will inevitably result from his policies of persistent deficit spending, and who flippantly replies to objections by stating "in the long run we're all dead" —or any other similar act of denying disagreeable truths, irrationality is, always and everywhere, a policy of trying to defraud reality.

Irrationality is: "the act of blanking out, the willful suspension of one's consciousness, the refusal to think—not blindness, but the refusal to see; not ignorance, but the refusal to know."[5]

Consider the difference between evasion and honest mistake. In *Atlas Shrugged,* for example, Hank Rearden mistakenly holds the premise of subjectivism. He repudiates the moral code of altruism but believes that there is no way for him to condemn the altruistic code of others. His innocent error causes him psychological torture. Because he fails to understand the objectivity of moral judgments, he voluntarily carries on his back evil men who seek his destruction. If he is to find the happiness he deserves, he must rectify this moral premise; an unwillingness to do so will perpetuate chronic agony.

Rearden is merely honestly mistaken; he is not an evader. He seeks to further his knowledge, including of moral principles. He tries to explain the observed facts, not shunt them aside. This is the reason he is able to learn a new moral code from Francisco and Galt, as well as from Dagny. In time, as a result of continued thinking, he realizes his error; he recognizes that moral principles are as objective as scientific ones. He throws off the slavery-inducing shackles of subjectivism, identifies the evil of the looters and moochers he has carried, and liberates himself from bondage to them.

If Rearden had not questioned the meaning of the looters' actions—if he had clung stubbornly to subjectivism's destructive teachings and pushed aside the rational principles of the strikers, refusing to consider them—then his life would have ended in tormented anguish, not in the joy of productive achievement. Facing bitter truths, not evading them, is the only way to ameliorate painful situations.

To take a different example: suppose a man's initial response to a new acquaintance is negative—he dislikes him, for whatever reason. But because he is inexorably open to facts, he observes, over time, that his initial negativity is unfounded: he comes to eventually see that the individual in question is honest, hard-working, trustworthy—and his erroneous original appraisal is identified and reversed. An honest mistake must be sharply distinguished from evasion.

To fully understand the revolutionary nature of Objectivism's commitment to rationality, it is necessary to contrast Ayn Rand's system with the two philosophical creeds dominant in the Western world: religion and materialism.

The Christians (or religionists more broadly) hold that faith, not reason, is the means by which man comes to know life's deepest truths. Faith is the uncritical acceptance of beliefs that not only have no evidence to support them—but worse, that fly in the face of all rational evidence. The starting point of such a "method" is generally a revealed text, such as the *Bible, Koran, Upanishads*, etc., the claims of which are accepted unquestioningly by believers. By such a non-rational method, any claim—no matter how bizarre or fantastic—may be embraced, including that men live inside whales, women are turned into pillars of salt, virgins give birth, corpses buried for days are revitalized, etc.

The method of reason begins with the direct observation of nature, and proceeds by asking questions that seek logical explanations of the observable facts. Faith, on the other hand, neither starts with observation of facts nor asks questions of "sacred beliefs." Its adherence to "revealed truth" is blind.

Because of its departure from reality, faith can lead only to destruction in human life. A paraphrase of Jesus states that "with sufficient faith you can move mountains." But, in fact, all the faith in the world is insufficient to move one grain of sand so much as one millimeter on a mountain. But with dynamite, i.e., with technology, science, reason, you can move mountains.

A vivid example of the dangerous, anti-reason nature of faith is provided by faith-healing denominations, who repudiate medical science. Faith healers, believing that prayer is the means to cure disease, eschew medical intervention, leaving them helpless before fatal but treatable ailments. One tragic result is numerous deaths from untreated diabetes, including those of children. In the religious era of the Dark and Middle Ages, before the rise of modern science and medicine, men prayed for succor from such killers as the bubonic plague—and died by the millions. Religion, subordinating reason to faith, rejects man's survival instrument, thereby leaving men no means by which to survive.

Materialism, the other dominant creed of the modern Western world, claims to be different. It upholds atheism and pretends to be "scientific." Nevertheless, Marx and his contemporary heirs (one although by no means the only prominent example of modern materialism) also reject the mind, though in a different form. Their belief is that nothing exists but matter, and that all human thoughts and emotions are reducible to electrical discharges and neural firings, i.e., bodily processes. As materialists, the Marxists hold that manual labor—the work of the body—is responsible for value creation and economic production.

Ayn Rand does not deride manual labor, which is a necessary component of any constructive activity. But she denies both the claim that thinking is reducible to bodily activities and its corollary, that intellectual work is reducible to manual labor. She argues that the intellectual work inherent in value creation is logically prior to, and significantly more difficult than, the physical labor. For example, before men could perform the tasks of carpentry, shingling, etc., necessary to build a house, somebody with knowledge of the principles of architecture and engineering had to design it. Similarly, electricians are skilled workers performing invaluable tasks, but their productive work is predicated on a genius like Thomas Edison creating the electric lighting system.

(Further, as discussed above, so-called "manual labor"—certainly that performed in a modern, industrialized society—is fundamentally intellectual work; electricians, plumbers, construction workers, et. al., do not toil like so many plow horses or oxen; unlike such beasts, they perform skilled work requiring knowledge. Even a ditch-digger must understand questions regarding how deep, how long, in what amount of time, etc.)

In effect, Ayn Rand asks contemporary materialists: how much manual labor did it take to invent the lighting system—or the airplane—or the personal computer and the Internet? How many physical workers toiling how many hours with how many pick-axes and shovels to discover a cure for polio—to identify the laws of thermo-dynamics—to formulate the theory of evolution—to compose Beethoven's symphonies—to write *Hamlet* or *War and Peace*? Her answer, of course, is that the question is not applicable. No amount of manual labor will suffice to reach those intellectual achievements. Fundamentally, these, and many others, are accomplishments of the mind.

There is no misfortune in having a national holiday named Labor Day—but, based on Ayn Rand's principles, we can ask: why is there no holiday named Men of the Mind Day? Or: Inventors' Day? Or: Entrepreneurs' and Industrialists' Day? Since it is the rational mind that fundamentally carries us forward, it is proper and just that America have a holiday celebrating those who exercise it and produce illustrious intellectual achievements.

Observe that Marx's theory, denying the efficacy (even the existence) of the mind, led to Communist dictatorships in which the best thinkers were permitted no freedom to disagree with the state, to create new knowledge or to revolutionize men's thinking in any field. The result was economic stagnation and collapse. There was (and remains) no shortage of whip-driven manual labor in the Soviet Union, Cuba or North Korea, but it is not sufficient to raise men's living standards above the starvation level. When all the independent minds of a society are stifled by a dictatorship, progress in that society grinds to a halt. The mind is the fundamental creator of all human values.

Since reason is man's instrument of survival, his commitment to it must be unflagging and inviolate. This is THE LESSON of Objectivism. What will be seen throughout this book is that regarding every question, issue, and problem of human life—from ethics to science to art to politics—Ayn Rand upholds man's rational mind as his sole method of gaining knowledge and his only proper guide to action. Every theoretical question must, can, and will be answered by reason; every practical action must be guided by man's mind and must respect the fact that man's mind is his survival instrument. This principle, called herein the lesson, is the theme that unifies Ayn Rand's thinking into a comprehensive system of philosophy.

The fundamental questions of human life, and consequently, of a philosophy capable of guiding men to success and happiness, regard the nature of the universe and of man's means of gaining knowledge. Once human beings have answers to these questions—and only then—is it logically possible to ask and answer: What should I do? What is morally right?

For example: if a man answers the foundational questions in the religious terms that the universe is created and governed by an all-powerful God, and that faith in the Bible is the means of understanding life's important truths, then the matter of what he should do is clear: he should obey God.

Or, alternatively: if he answers the basic questions in the materialist terms that all things—men included—are composed exclusively of matter, and that knowledge is gained by following his visceral urges and impulses, then, again, what he should do is clear: he should live for the hedonistic gratification of his bodily desires.

The issues of metaphysics and epistemology are of paramount importance to human life. We know that Ayn Rand upholds an unbreached commitment to rationality as the sole means of gaining knowledge. What theory does she hold regarding the nature of reality?

Chapter 5

The Universe as an Intelligible Natural System

A brief study of history and current events show that men have made great improvements in their lives on earth. They have invented automobiles, airplanes, and computers, cured innumerable diseases, built skyscrapers and cities, and significantly raised their living standards and life expectancies. As has been discussed, the faculty enabling men to deal effectively with reality and reach such achievements is: reason. Successful living in reality requires men to adhere to facts, to the truth—no matter how painful or unpleasant—and to never evade.

But what does it mean to adhere to the facts of reality? What is reality? Does adherence to reality mean to identify and live in accordance with nature's laws—to obey God—to conform to society—or some eclectic mixture of these? The preceding chapters have suggested that, for Ayn Rand, reality consists fundamentally of nature; there is no supernatural dimension. Although there is a social world, to uncritically conform to the ideas of other men is as destructive as blind compliance to the fantasies of supernaturalism. According to Objectivism, adherence to reality means one thing: fidelity to the facts and laws of the natural world. Rationality, man's mind, is a faculty for understanding—and achieving flourishing life in—the secular, natural world. Ayn Rand's reasons for this must be made clear.

The branch of philosophy that answers such questions is: metaphysics—the study of the nature of the universe as such. Ayn Rand holds that a rational metaphysics consists of one fundamental principle: Existence—and its corollaries: Identity, Causality, Consciousness.

The first point to be made is: *Existence exists.* A rational philosophy starts with the most fundamental point. Looking out at the world, at any aspect of it—in this case, at a computer—we say: this *is*. Looking out the window, at the trees, buildings, and automobiles in the distance, we say: these things *are*. Something exists.

"We start with the irreducible fact and concept of existence—that which is.

This realization is the starting point of all cognition. Prior to any subsequent question, before one can even seek to identify what *kinds* of things there are—before any further learning takes place, there must first be something to be learned and one must know this basic fact. "If not, there is nothing to consider or to know."[1]

Related: there is no non-existence, no realm of nothingness to serve as an alternative or competitor to existence. The Greek philosopher, Parmenides, stated this point succinctly: "what is, is; what is not, is not." There is no realm of non-being—a contradiction in terms—out of which things are created or into which they are banished. The things that exist can and do change their forms—but existence as such can be neither created nor destroyed. Existence exists—and only existence exists.

A corollary of Existence is: Identity. This principle states that a thing is what it is—and is not what it is not. Symbolically: A is A—and it is not non-A. For any existent, to be is to be *something*. "Whatever you choose to consider, be it an object, an attribute or an action, the law of identity remains the same. A leaf cannot be a stone at the same time, it cannot be all red and all green at the same time, it cannot freeze and burn at the same time."[2]

Ayn Rand does not hold that existence *has* identity, as if the latter were an aspect distinguishable from the former, as clothes are separable from the individual wearing them. Rather, existence *is* identity—it is impossible to divide a thing's existence from its nature. A cat, for example, is a cat—a single indivisible whole. It is not the case that there is an entity—a cat—and a set of characteristics—claws, teeth, effectiveness as a mouser, etc.—distinguishable from the entity as a separable feature. "If something *exists*, then *something* exists; and if there is a *something*, then there *is* a something."[3]

A second corollary is a straightforward derivative from Ayn Rand's primaries: the Law of Causality. This principle states: in any given set of circumstances, a thing can act in one way and only one way—in accordance with its nature. The law of causality is simply the law of identity applied to action. The way in which entities behave in a specific milieu is a product of the identity relationships involved. For example: suppose a tiny ice cube is tossed into an Olympic sized swimming pool whose water is heated to eighty degrees. What will happen? The ice cube will melt and, so doing, will lower the water temperature by a minute amount. Is there any possibility of the ice cube behaving differently under the circumstances? None. Given the identities of the ice and of the warm water, the outcome was inescapable. Similarly, if a crow bar is thrown into the water, it will sink—and a cork will float. Given the nature of such entities, there is no other course of action open to them in such a context.

An entity cannot act in defiance of its nature. A dog cannot fly, rubber cannot replace steel in the construction of skyscrapers, and sulfuric acid cannot function as cough syrup. "A thing cannot act apart from its nature, because existence *is* identity; apart from its nature, a thing is nothing." Action flows from nature—what a thing is determines what it can do. Because existence is identity, causality is universal. The law of causality is a corollary of the law of identity: it is self-evident upon grasping the principle of identity, i.e., nothing else is necessary to comprehend its truth.[4]

Every existent is something and, consequently, necessarily acts in accordance with its nature. Because of this, the universe is a vast network of interlocking identity relationships, i.e., of causal patterns composed of entities acting as they must. The sun, for example, given its nature, exerts a gravitational attraction on the earth, which, given its nature, must revolve around it, completing an elliptical orbit in the time it takes to rotate fully on its axis three hundred and sixty-five times. This is merely one of the myriad causal relationships constituting the universe, the sum of existents.

But the human capacity to sense that something exists and to later identify the nature of those somethings involves another fundamental aspect of reality: that men possess the faculty of *consciousness*. "Existence exists—and the act of grasping that statement implies two corollary axioms: that something exists which one perceives and that one exists possessing consciousness, consciousness being the faculty of perceiving that which exists." (It should be noted that consciousness is not a corollary of existence as such; it is perfectly possible for the universe to exist with no consciousness present within it. Rather, consciousness is inherent in *comprehending* the fact of existence.)[5]

An individual may be aware of the smell of food, of a television show, of the sound of passing cars in the street, etc. The awareness may be visual or auditory (or of another sense modality), perceptual or conceptual, but in some form consciousness requires an object, something to be aware of. A consciousness conscious of nothing is an impossibility—for the question is: *consciousness* of what? Similarly, a consciousness conscious of nothing but itself is also impossible. It could not identify itself as consciousness if it were not antecedently aware of some other object(s). It could not be consciousness in the absence of some independent reality to be aware of, for the question would simply arise in a slightly altered form: consciousness of consciousness—of *what*? (This is why babies must sense external stimuli for many months before beginning to develop self-awareness.) "If that which you claim to perceive does not exist, what you possess is not consciousness."[6]

Each of these four basic principles is involved in every item of knowledge possessed by any mind at any time—from the earliest perception of a child to the most complex theory developed by a monumental genius. For example, a child throws a ball and sees it roll on the carpet. To make the point simply, first: there is something that he throws (and someone who throws it)—Existence. There is a specific *something* that is thrown, a ball—Identity. The ball rolls on the carpet *because* it is round—Causality. The child sees the ball with his eyes, hears it hit the floor with his ears, and comes to understand with his mind that the act of throwing will cause the ball to move away—Consciousness.

Observe an important point regarding the relationship between these principles: consciousness is a means of cognizing or understanding reality, not of creating or altering it. Consciousness has no means to directly control existence. It cannot, by a sheer act of itself, bring objects into existence or expunge those that do exist; nor can it by the same means alter the nature of an existent. "From the outset, consciousness presents itself as something specific—as a faculty of perceiving an object, not of creating or changing it." For example, a child might hate the vegetables he has to eat, and desire them to be ice cream—but no amount of wishing on his part deletes the detested foods from existence or transforms them into the favored one. In a rudimentary, implicit form, consonant with their preliminary state of knowledge, children grasp early on that no direct act of consciousness—no wishing, willing, hating, aspiring, etc.—can affect the existence or nature of independently existing things. Existence is impervious to any act of awareness; existence, in short, has primacy over consciousness.[7]

Ayn Rand's revolutionary "primacy of existence" principle identifies the relationship between these two fundamental axioms of human cognition. Existence is logically prior. Because consciousness requires an object, it is a metaphysical dependent; it cannot stand alone; its only power is to become aware of that which exists. Existence is fundamental, foundational, and independent of consciousness—any consciousness. It requires nothing and depends on nothing. In a classic formulation, Ayn Rand expresses the basis of all reality-based thought. "Existence is Identity, Consciousness is Identification."[8]

Historically, Francis Bacon provided an aphorism that can be employed to brilliantly specify the essentials of Ayn Rand's metaphysics: "Nature, to be commanded, must be obeyed." Bacon pointed out that nature is the elemental, not-to-be-challenged term setter to which all cognition must comply. If men identify, acknowledge, and accede to nature's laws, they gain knowledge and thereby the power to improve their lives. But if they ignore, flout, or defy nature's laws, they suffer; if they do so egregiously, they perish. In other words, recognition of the primacy of existence principle, consistently applied, is the starting point of an inviolable commitment to reason.

Related, Bacon's aphorism identifies another point congruent with Ayn Rand's fundamentals: a proper metaphysics identifies the fact and fundamentality of existence—but, in and of itself, catalogs neither the types of existents and the causal laws that govern them nor the means by which men must re-fashion what exists in order to promote their lives. All of these specific facts and principles men must gradually discover. It is the function of other cognitive disciplines—including the sciences—to accomplish this, and they can do so only by scrupulous adherence to the primacy of existence principle.

Ayn Rand calls the opposite of this theory "the primacy of consciousness" metaphysics. It holds that consciousness, in some form, creates and governs existence. Consciousness is the fundamental reality and existence depends on it. "In this view, the function of consciousness is not perception, but creation of that which is. Existence, accordingly, is a dependent; the world is regarded as in some way a derivative of consciousness."[9]

A story attributed to Abraham Lincoln serves to illustrate the distinction between these two metaphysical approaches. Addressing a backwoods audience, Lincoln purportedly asked the crowd: "If we call a horse's tail 'a leg,' how many legs will the horse then have?" The audience promptly answered: "Five." "No," Lincoln replied. "The horse will have four legs, because calling a tail 'a leg' will not make it so." On a primacy of consciousness premise, if a mind (or a group of them) designates a tail a leg, then reality somehow bends to its wishes. But the primacy of existence theory recognizes that reality is not subordinate to a mere act of consciousness, but remains immutable despite the will, wish, hope or desire of some mind (or group of them).

The primacy of consciousness theory represents the fundamental error in metaphysics—and, historically, religion is the distilled essence of this misconceived approach. On this view, dominant in the West's medieval period and in the contemporary Islamic world, an alleged supernatural consciousness—a cosmic spirit of total power—creates the entire universe from nothing. Since God creates the world, He governs it and can will anything He wishes. So, for example, burning bushes speak, virgins give birth, men dead and buried for days are revitalized, etc. No action, regardless of how egregiously it violates the Law of Identity, is beyond the capacity of the all-powerful creator and governor of the universe. Religion, the *supernatural* version of the primacy of consciousness metaphysics, postulates that consciousness *literally creates* the universe.

The practical results, in human life, are disastrous. If men believe that a supernatural consciousness controls reality, then it follows that its all-powerful will is the sole determiner of right and wrong—and it can be accessed only by the ineffable methods of faith and prayer. So, for example, if God commands men to make war on the "infidels," then His will must be carried out (as Christians and Muslims, as well as other sects have often done.) If God opposes the use of medicine, as faith healing denominations maintain, then their members will eschew medical cures, seek to heal illness by means of prayer, and suffer vastly lower life expectancies as a result. If God's word, as presented in the Bible, must be taken literally, as Fundamentalists claim, then the theory of evolution must be repudiated as arrant blasphemy.

In politics, theocratic dictatorships of the type perpetrated by the medieval Catholic Church and the contemporary Islamists (e.g., in Iran and recently in Afghanistan) are the logical consequence of such a metaphysics; for the clergy, i.e., the initiated spiritual elite—those expert at interpreting the will of the ruling consciousness—are the only ones theologically and morally qualified to ensure that the legal system conforms to God's commandments. The result of subordinating the rational requirements of men's lives to the fantasy of God's will is the Dark Age of medieval Europe, a similar dark age in recent Afghanistan (under the Taliban), and the brutal tyranny of contemporary Iran (under the ayatollahs). On a supernatural version of the primacy of consciousness approach, reason—man's tool of survival—is necessarily abrogated in favor of faith.

In the 18th and 19th centuries, the influential German philosophers, Immanuel Kant and G.W.F. Hegel, secularized the religious view. In everyday parlance, the phrase, "Fifty million Frenchmen can't be wrong," captures the meaning of their theory. Why can't fifty million human beings be wrong? Because, on this *social version of the primacy of consciousness approach*, the human mind, by means of its basic innate structure—the inherent means by which men engage in cognition—constructs the reality it experiences. The group, on this view, society as a whole, imposes its core beliefs on raw sensory data to create the world as we know it, the "human world." "Truth," the moderns say, "is socially constructed."

After all, if reality existed independently of men's experience—if it is not created by their minds—then millions of individuals could be as mistaken as one. But if the fundamental beliefs of a society were the cognitive term setters—if they shaped and conditioned what was held to be reality within that society—then society as a whole could be no more in error than could God.

For example, on this theory, if primitive tribes held that diseases were caused by evil spirits and cured by the incantations of witch doctors, then such beliefs were true in those societies and thereby formed the reality within which those peoples lived. Similarly, if medieval Christians interpreted plagues as God's wrath visited upon sinful man, the solution being a return to "righteousness" (i.e., unquestioning obedience), then such fundamental concepts formed the essence of their reality. Continuing the same theme, if modern Western men construe germs as the cause of disease and antibiotics as the cure, then, according to the social primacy of consciousness theory, these ideas condition the reality that they occupy—but not the reality of other groups.

Several popular sayings current in American culture express this theory. One is that "perception is reality." The other is that "image is everything." The meaning of each is that the fundamental truth regarding "x"—whatever value is substituted for the variable—is that which the majority within a society believes about it. Truth, on this view, is social. If a claim is true *because* society believes it, then social belief is like God's will (on the supernaturalist approach); social belief shapes reality, which is subordinate to it.

In *The Fountainhead,* Howard Roark protests against this theory. He states: "Why is anyone and everyone right—so long as it's not yourself? Why does the number of those others take the place of truth? Why is truth made a mere matter of arithmetic—and only of addition at that?" His objection, of course, is that a claim is not true merely because most (or all) members of society uphold it. For example, if all men held that the earth was the center of (what would then be) a "geo-system" and that the sun revolved around it, their belief would be woefully insufficient to make it so.[10]

The political consequences of the social school of the primacy of consciousness theory are powerful—and lethal. The theory is: if the people will it, then reality snaps into line. Therefore, if the Aryan people (or their political leaders—the National Socialist Workers Party of Germany, the Nazis) collectively will (or sense or desire or viscerally feel) their moral superiority based on biological inheritance, then it is so. Similarly, if (according to the Khmer Rouge) the Cambodian proletariat collectively wills it possible to convert jungle into productive agricultural land, then—despite the soil's unsuitability—it can be done. The Chinese Communist dictator, Mao Tse-tung, for example, "did not believe in 'objective situations' at all." Rather, he believed in the power of man's will to bend the world to its design. Presumably, on his view, if the masses willed it, they could fly across the Pacific by flapping their arms. That the will of the people (or race or nation or tribe or state) shapes reality is an article of faith for modern collectivists—and is an integral component of the National Socialist and Communist ideologies that wrought such murderous havoc in the 20th century. On the social version of this deadly metaphysical error, reason is dispensed with not in favor of faith in the supernatural—but in favor of faith in society, i.e., in favor of conformity to the group and obedience to its leaders.[11]

The third variation of this metaphysical theory is the *personal* version. This involves the belief that if an individual claims "x" to be true, then it is so for him. Reality is malleable and adapts itself to the whim of each person. So, for example, if the true believer holds, with the poet Robert Browning, that "God's in His Heaven, All's right with the world," then it is so—for him. At the same time, if the atheist holds that there is no God, then, again, it is so—for him. On this version of the primacy of consciousness theory, as on the others, existence is infinitely alterable, dominated by the will of the ruling consciousness.

This version also has lethal consequences. For example, the drug user is on the implicit assumption that somehow the cocaine, heroin or other toxic substance(s) that he imbibes will fail to harm him if only he fervently desires his indulgence to be innocuous. On the view that the true (or the right) for me is whatever I hold or desire, any conviction—no matter how self-destructive or murderous—can be validated. To paraphrase Dostoyevsky while utterly reversing his meaning: in a world without the primacy of existence principle, all things become permissible. On a personal version of the primacy of consciousness metaphysics, reason is abandoned for emotionalism, hedonism, and wanton, unrestrained self-indulgence.

Any form of the primacy of consciousness theory obliterates commitment to the metaphysical absolutism of existence and replaces it with obedience to an imaginary ruling consciousness. The logical result is that fantasy, in various forms, replaces reality as the ruling concern of men's lives, leaving men bereft of an effectual means to deal with the world. Reason, man's tool of survival, involves an unflagging commitment to reality—not to the will of some consciousness (real or imaginary) held to supersede it. The subordination of existence to consciousness necessitates a concomitant subordination of reason to whim worship in some form. This is the deeper reason that religion, collectivism, and emotionalism lead only to destruction in human life.

A related error: today many people believe and loudly proclaim that "there are no absolutes." This belief states that no principle is universally truthful, that there are exceptions to every rule, and that reality is malleable. Based on the fundamentals of a rational metaphysics, the falsity of such a belief becomes clear. Is the law of gravity, for example, a non-absolute? Are there moments when its operation is held in abeyance—and a man can leap off of the Empire State Building and float suspended in space? Obviously not. A man may wish it so—but, in fact, such an attraction between bodies exists, it is what it is, it functions inexorably, and its nature can be understood but not altered by man's mind. The laws of nature are absolute. "Absolute," in this context means: "necessitated by the nature of existence and, therefore, unchangeable by human (or any other) agency."

Indeed, all of what Ayn Rand terms the "metaphysically given" is absolute in this sense. The metaphysically given, she states, is all of that which exists independent of human choice or action. It is distinguished from man-made facts, which are entities, relationships, policies, institutions, etc., established by human choice. For example: the sun is metaphysically given; solar panels are man-made. The law of gravity is metaphysically given; the laws against violent crime are man-made. Germs are metaphysically given; antibiotics are man-made.

An innumerable array of facts are metaphysically given absolutes. To cite a tiny sample: the sun warms the earth. Human beings require food to survive. Cats are carnivores. Germs cause disease. Water is necessary for life. The mind is man's means of survival. Metaphysically given facts *are reality*. They are simply to be accepted; not to be evaluated, acclaimed, criticized, challenged or rejected, but acknowledged.

Man can *rearrange* the elements of nature (not create them from nothing-ness) in order to further his life, e.g., he can introduce water from elsewhere into a barren desert by means of irrigation in order to grow crops. But he can do this only by enacting the appropriate cause, i.e., the one dictated by the inalterable laws of reality. In this case, to transform a barren desert into fertile land it is necessary to transport water into the area; in the absence of introducing water, the land remains incapable of sustaining life. *Human beings must acknowledge nature's laws as a necessary condition of rearranging nature's specific elements.* Therefore, human creativity is not an abrogation of the absolutism of reality, but the opposite. "In order to succeed, [man's] actions must conform to the metaphysically given."

The man-made, on the other hand, is not an immutable fixture of reality. It is a product of choice, and, as such, subject to evaluation, criticism, approval or rejection. To paraphrase a widely-held falsehood and reverse its meaning: "You *can* fight city hall." (Indeed, in support of your life, sometimes you must.) Human beings can err, whether honestly or dishonestly, and their judgments are sometimes false and to be rejected. Nature, to be revised, must necessarily be accepted—but nothing that is man-made possesses this metaphysical status. The law of gravitation, for example, simply is—and if men are to achieve flight, they must accept its absolutism and work within these parameters. But a law of Congress is not part of the changeless given of reality. If Congress (or any legislative body) imposes laws inimical to men's lives, as it unfortunately sometimes does, men do not have to accept them and then struggle for life under crippling social conditions. Rather, they can and should repudiate such laws, speak out against them, and elect candidates who will reverse them in favor of ones that respect men's right to live.[12]

As a final example, the widely held belief that "nothing is inevitable but death and taxes" must be understood as a misconception: death is inevitable; taxes are not.

The laws of nature, but not of man, are timelessly inalterable, not-to-be-challenged absolutes.

Putting reality above and ahead of any other consideration, i.e., adopting the primacy of existence approach, is the essence of a rational life. On such a method, for example, cocaine is rejected in favor of clean living—even if an individual experiences self-destructive urges—because, *in fact*, it is lethal. Similarly, faith healing is repudiated, because *the facts of reality* establish that diseases are caused by germs, not man's sin, and are expunged by medicine, not by prayer. A final example: legally (and morally), justice must be blind to all considerations but the *facts* of a specific case; to ensure that justice is served, the morally upright man ruthlessly excises his own personal feelings (or faith or beliefs of others, etc.) from assessment of a case, focusing exclusively on its factual merits.

Existence, Identity, Causality, and Consciousness—these are the four foundational principles of metaphysics. The truth of these basic concepts—and of their corollary primacy of existence principle—constitutes the base of Objectivism. These foundational principles provide the deepest reasons that men must choose to be rational—and thereby explicate more fully The Lesson of Objectivism. As such, this foundation has an important implication regarding the successful pursuit of knowledge and values.

Because things are what they are, they are discernible by man's mind. Because existence is universally lawful, it is universally intelligible. Every entity and action is accessible to man's rational awareness. It only remains for man to identify the specific governing laws. To access nature's lawful patterns and thereby discover how to achieve life-promoting values, human beings must follow reason. To follow reason, in Ayn Rand's philosophy, means to choose to employ a cognitive method that subordinates all other considerations to a reverence for the facts of reality. Man must enact an intellectual method consonant with the primacy of existence principle. To be successful, in other words, he must learn and then choose to be objective.

Chapter 6

Objectivity as the Method of Rational Cognition

The questions of morality (and of philosophy more broadly) are so abstract and difficult that many people in the modern world regard them as unanswerable. Certainly, a dominant contemporary view is that philosophy is merely a matter of opinion; that philosophical "truth" varies from society to society—and even from individual to individual; that philosophy is subjective, not objective—and contrasts, in this regard, with mathematics and the sciences.

Here then is the cognitive alternative generally offered to modern man: religion says truths in morality and philosophy are possible—but only if one has faith. The contemporary secular intellectuals who control the universities, the educational system, and the media reject faith and, with it, truth, certainty, and knowledge. One popular version of the modernist view is the theory of multiculturalism, which claims that truth varies from culture to culture—that an individual is indoctrinated by the society in which he's raised—that he necessarily absorbs its specific views and general frame of reference, thereby making it impossible for him to understand or evaluate differing cultures—and that a belief in objective truth is merely a "white Western male" prejudice.

Multiculturalism is merely one version of the modern view originated and propagated by the German philosophers Immanuel Kant and G.W.F. Hegel. Following these two thinkers, modern intellectuals maintain that man confronts the world with specific ideas, categories, concepts, theories, hopes, beliefs, desires or prejudices already mentally (consciously or subconsciously) operative, thereby causing the mind to mold incoming observational data in accordance with its own subjective elements. Consequently, the human mind can never comprehend reality as it "really is"; it can never know "things in themselves," as Kant termed it; it can know only the distorted version it itself creates. Human beings can therefore never gain objective truth, i.e., knowledge of objects that exist independent of human consciousness.

Ayn Rand utterly repudiates both the school of modern subjectivism and the

47

religious theory. She abjures equally the modernist claim that objective knowledge is impossible and the religious view that to reach objective truths requires faith. Reason, not faith, is the exclusive means to gain truth; and the mind's specific nature, far from preventing men from reaching truth, is what makes it possible. Objective knowledge is gained solely by the application of a *distinctively human method of cognition* to the facts of reality.

Indeed, the principle of objectivity is central to Ayn Rand's thought, which is why she named her philosophy: Objectivism. She advocates objectivity in all branches of cognition, including all areas and questions of philosophy, and holds that—when properly arrived at, i.e., when reached by a rational process—philosophical conclusions are as objective as those in mathematics or the sciences. Ayn Rand's objective approach to knowledge and philosophy has been implicit throughout the first five chapters of this book—and it is now time to explicitly identify her reasons. Why did Ayn Rand hold that objectivity is possible in philosophy, as in all cognitive disciplines—and what is the method that makes it actual?

Objectivity, Ayn Rand held, is both a metaphysical and an epistemological concept. Metaphysically, objectivity rests on the unconditional acceptance of the fundamental fact of reality: existence has primacy over consciousness. Or, in Ayn Rand's own words, the metaphysical aspect of objectivity involves "recognition of the fact that reality exists independent of any perceiver's consciousness."[1]

Existence sets the terms of cognition; therefore, men must adhere to it in order to gain knowledge. That is, they must be fact-oriented or reality-based in approach. In everyday usage, the phrase that perfectly captures this idea was famously stated in the old *Dragnet* television series: "Just give us the facts, ma'am." Since the heroes were detectives, it was imperative they receive from witnesses neither hysteria nor emotionalist evaluations—but the unvarnished observational data, i.e., just the facts. Given the truth of the primacy of existence principle, such an approach is a matter of life and death for all human beings, not merely for detectives.

However, the primacy of consciousness approach, in all of its versions and manifestations, abrogates this metaphysical aspect of objectivity. Whether in the form of religion, collectivism, or personal whim worship, the primacy of consciousness school subordinates existence to the wishes and arbitrary decrees of an alleged "ruling consciousness." Such an approach eliminates the foundation and very possibility of objectivity, guaranteeing that its adherents will, in some form, enshrine whims and devalue facts.

It has often been observed that men are neither infallible nor omniscient; that they commit errors. Often overlooked is that the primacy of existence principle represents the deepest reason for this. Because existence is the primary factor, consciousness, in order to gain knowledge, must adhere to it; when consciousness fails to adhere to existence, it thereby commits a fundamental error. But if the primacy of consciousness theory, in any of its variations, were true, the ruling consciousness would be incapable of error (just as religion holds God to be). Since, on such a view, consciousness creates and/or controls reality, it would merely need to wish or decree—and *voila*, reality would immediately bow in compliance.

But, since in fact consciousness must adhere to reality, men must discover nature's laws and specific facts. Since reality, not man, sets the standard of truth, men may fail—deliberately or unwittingly—to meet that standard. They might commit factual errors, e.g., believe that sailing across the ocean will lead them to plunge off the world's edge. Or: they might formulate theories that fail to accurately explain observational data, e.g., believe that diseases are caused by evil spirits or human sinfulness or an imbalance of bodily fluids (or "humors") rather than by germs.

To ascertain the truth (and to correct any such errors) human beings need to consistently practice an existence-oriented method, and eschew every form of abrogating it. They must repudiate supernaturalism, i.e., metaphysical fantasy, as well as social conformity and personal whim worship. They need to expunge from their thinking all manifestations of a primacy of consciousness approach.

As an epistemological principle, objectivity requires that men enact a specific cognitive method in the quest to gain knowledge. Objectivity "is the recognition of the fact that a perceiver's...consciousness must acquire knowledge of reality by certain means (reason) in accordance with certain rules (logic)." The question of epistemology is of method: How—by what specific means—does a rational consciousness adhere to existence?[2]

It is important in this context to contrast the cognitive methods of perception and conception. At the perceptual (or observational) level, consciousness automatically adheres to reality. For example, the sun's rays strike a person's skin, and he feels warmth—or vibrating air molecules impinge on his ears, and he hears sound—or light beams reflect off of objects and hit his eyes, and he sees a room full of furniture. In short, perception is an automatic process rigidly controlled by the laws of physics—and contains, consequently, no possibility of deviating from reality.

But this is not the case at the conceptual level. Here, in the realm of ideas, principles, theories, and interpretations of observational data, people often err. Indeed, the history of human cognition is littered with discarded theories, held as gospel truth in one era but subsequently invalidated. For example, at one time men believed that the earth was the center of the universe and that the sun revolved around it. At various times, they have held that moral characteristics are biologically transmittable (the Nazis)—that superior beings reside on the summit of Mt. Olympus (the ancient Greeks)—that the earth was mere thousands of years old and that man was created in a single day (religious Fundamentalists). But all of these (at one-time) widespread beliefs were later proven false.

True theories or explanatory principles in any field—from architecture to zoology—do not strike men's minds in the manner that light rays strike their eyes. At this level, in contrast with the level of perception, human consciousness can err. What is the fundamental cause of human fallibility? Why has the history of knowledge inevitably been a tortuous process, struggling upward from repeated errors to eventual apprehensions of truth? Because, in Ayn Rand's words, man is a being of volitional consciousness; because the truth of the primacy of existence principle obviates the possibility that an idea—simply because it is held by consciousness—automatically, self-certifiably adheres to reality. At the intellectual level, in order to reach truth, human beings must engage in *voluntary* mental work that does not *automatically* achieve accurate theoretical understanding. Nothing can or will alter this basic metaphysical truth.

Therefore, the fundamental task of philosophy is epistemological, i.e., involves ascertaining the means by which men gain conceptual knowledge. Philosophy's central purpose is to identify and explain the fundamental steps, the processes, the rules a conceptual consciousness must follow to adhere to the facts.

To gain knowledge at the intellectual level, men need a proper cognitive method—and they must choose to enact it. Intellectual knowledge *"is the grasp of an object through an active, reality-based process chosen by the subject."* The question is: by what method can a fallible being achieve truth, knowledge, certainty? The method is: logic. It is the method by which a volitional consciousness adheres to reality. Aristotle, not Ayn Rand, was the father of logic. But Ayn Rand provided the critical definition: logic is the art of non-contradictory identification. (And she made significant contributions in this field, as discussed below.)[3]

To understand an object is to *identify* it, to discover its nature, its essence, its identity. All questions raised by the mind involve: "What is it?" If men ask, for example, "Why did an occurrence take place?" it means, "What is the nature of the cause?" If they ask, "How did it occur?" it means, "What is the nature of the process?" If they inquire, "Where did it happen?" the question means, "What is the place?" The role of consciousness is exclusively to discover the identity of the things that exist.[4]

The law of identity thereby sets the task of consciousness, acting as a bridge between existence and consciousness, between the principles of metaphysics and those of epistemology. The law leads to the fundamental rule of intellectual cognition: to be reality-based, any identification must be non-contradictory. Aristotle's justly famous law of non-contradiction states that a thing cannot be both A and non-A at the same time and in the same respect. (Obviously, such a principle is a corollary of the law of identity: A is A.) So, for example, a thing may be red or non-red at different times or in different senses—but it cannot be both red and non-red at the same time and in the same sense. A thing cannot grow and shrink at the same time and in the same respect—it cannot be born and die at the same time and in the same sense—it cannot simultaneously fly and remain earthbound, etc.

Contradictions exist only in the minds of persons who are confused; there are and can be none in existence independent of consciousness. To hold a contradiction in one's thinking is to attempt to negate identity and thereby to defy the fundamental principle of existence. It represents the lethal intellectual error. To reach a contradiction, Ayn Rand stated, is to admit a mistake in one's cognition; "to maintain a contradiction is to abdicate one's mind and to evict oneself from the realm of reality."[5]

The law of non-contradiction is the defining essence of reality-based thought. "Whenever one moves by a volitional process from known data to a new cognition ostensibly based on these data, the ruling question must be: can the new cognition be integrated *without contradiction* into the sum of one's knowledge?" This is what it means to follow logic—the method of objective thought[6]

For example, the theory of evolution is still disputed by some religionists. The theory claims that all life forms on earth—including man, the most biologically sophisticated—developed over time from a single common ancestor. Does this idea integrate with what we know about the earth and about life? Research shows that it does indeed fit seamlessly into an extensive range of knowledge.

Geologists, for instance, estimate the age of the earth at roughly 4.65 billion years. Fossil records show life forms dating back to 3.5 billion years ago. In keeping with the theory that more complex life forms developed from simpler ones, the earliest fossil records are of bacteria. In keeping with the theory that life arose naturally from "pre-biotic chemical constituents," rocks that are 3.8 billion years old show "forms of carbon atoms (isotopes) considered by biochemists as a fingerprint of the presence of life." Fossil records show that for 1 billion years, life forms on earth were restricted to bacteria. Fossils also show that the earliest forms of animal life appeared roughly 535 million years in the past—and that the human lineage appeared only some 4 million years ago. There exists a gradation of "fossil human remains spanning the duration of the last 3 million years in Africa"—showing a steady, continuous development from apelike creatures to modern man. Further, advances in genetic science reveal the same RNA and DNA structure in all living forms—bacteria, fungi, plants, animals, man—powerful evidence for the claim of an interconnected line of biological descent.[7]

The theory of evolution integrates without contradiction a vast sum of empirical data identified by scientists in a wide range of fields—geology, paleontology, biochemistry, and genetics, to name only a few.

Additionally, its cognitive method is fact-based and naturalistic, making no transcendent references in the attempt to explain the genesis of human life; it thereby integrates more widely with the central philosophical truth that reason—not faith, feelings, or any similarly irrational "method"—is man's means of gaining knowledge and guiding successful life. Related, this means that evolutionary theory is consistent with the primacy of existence approach—and repudiates all forms of the primacy of consciousness error.

Is there any knowledge that contradicts the claims of evolution? None. All that opposes it is the explicit religious belief of creationism (or its camouflaged version—the theory of intelligent design.) But religious belief violates the fundamental principle of a rational metaphysics—the primacy of existence over consciousness—and must be dismissed from serious intellectual discussion.

The theory of evolution is thereby established by reference to the broad range of scientific and philosophical knowledge with which it coheres without contradiction. It forms a seamless part of an integrated rational view of existence.

Ayn Rand's unqualified endorsement of laissez-faire capitalism represents a second instance of non-contradictory integration. For example, prior to the capitalist revolution of the 18th century Enlightenment, Europeans lived under monarchical despotism and in miserable penury. But the principle of individual rights liberated commoners from bondage to the aristocrats, freed them to pursue their own happiness and to deploy their rational minds in that quest; freed them to advance in every field of human endeavor—including applied science and technology—and thereby enormously boosted both living standards and life expectancies.[8]

Further, her support of capitalism integrates not merely with historical knowledge but with the science of economics, which establishes that only the free market system is capable of creating a widespread abundance of consumer goods—and that statism of any form, emphatically including all types of socialism, leads necessarily to widespread destitution. One critical principle in this regard is that the freedom of the capitalist system liberates every man to employ his mind in the production of the values required by human life. When man's survival instrument is unrestrained, more men will survive, for longer periods of time, and at higher living standards.[9]

Above all, advocacy of capitalism coheres with the rational principles of philosophy that Ayn Rand herself identified. For example, because men need to egoistically achieve values in order to live, they must have the legal right to pursue them; therefore, the principle of individual rights, and a limited Constitutional government to protect such rights, is necessary. (See Chapter Eleven.) Related, since the mind is mankind's survival instrument, men must be free to apply their rational judgment to questions of practical life without need to gain permission, including that of the state. Virtue requires men to be consistently rational—and capitalism, by protecting each individual's inalienable right to employ his own mind, is the sole system that enables them to be so. (See Chapter Nine.) A final moral point: since (according to Objectivism) the good is that which promotes man's life on earth, capitalism, by enabling the explosion of creative, life-giving advances proceeding from the protection of men's right to their own lives and minds, is a good of virtually unprecedented historical proportions.(See Chapter Eight.)

Deeper, rationality (and its method of objectivity) are required of men because of the metaphysical truth of the primacy of existence principle. Capitalism—the sole system liberating men's rational minds—is thereby the sole system fully congruent with this deepest truth of reality. (See Chapters Five and Six.)

On the polemical side, the opposite of capitalism—statism in any of its manifestations—repeatedly violates the right of individuals to their own lives and minds, and consequently leads predictably to brutal repression, economic collapse, and mass murder.

In brief, Ayn Rand's full support of laissez-faire capitalism is the only conclusion that integrates without contradiction into an enormous body of knowledge from history, economics, ethics, and deeper philosophy.

By contrast, a cognitive claim that cannot be integrated without contradiction into the sum of a rational man's knowledge must be rejected. For example, an independent thinker will be led to question the continued apologia for Communism on the part of the Western intelligentsia. "Deaths under Stalin were greatly exaggerated," he hears—or "Ho Chi Minh was the George Washington of Vietnam"—or "Under Mao, at least every Chinese received a bowl of rice per day"—etc.

But, the rational thinker will realize, Communism holds that no individual possesses a right to his own life—and that each man must exist for the state. This, he recognizes, is a principle held in common with the Nazis. Further, like National Socialism, Communism is a totalitarian manifestation, with closed borders, suppressed intellectual expression, and concentration camps or gulags. People die seeking escape to the West, he knows, not vice-versa; indeed, they die merely for speaking their minds. Today, he might even be aware of state-of-the-art research into the archives of former Communist regimes revealing a numbing total of *100 million murders* in 80 years. Further, he's read (or remembers) that the brutal suppression led to severe economic collapse, to widespread famine, e.g., in Soviet Russia, China, and North Korea, and that massive food shipments from America and other freer nations were necessary to save lives.[10]

Finally, what about the fact that the mind is man's fundamental means of survival—that the mind requires freedom—and that when it is suppressed, as during the Dark Ages, progress ceases and men regress into hellishly primitive living conditions? He knows that under Communism rational thinkers are cruelly repressed—the Siberian exile of Nobel Prize winning physicist, Andrei Sakharov, constitutes but one example—so that, with the cause of progress stifled, claims of intellectual and material advance under such a system amount to nothing but arrant propaganda.

Therefore, the claims that Communism is (in whole or in part) benign are incongruent with a wide context of knowledge. This body of knowledge integrates only with pro-freedom arguments that indict Communism as a system of the cruelest tyranny leading inevitably to terror, repression, extermination, enslavement, bloody conquest, and severe economic destitution. He concludes properly that claims supporting the benevolence of Communism contradict an entire body of knowledge regarding both collectivism's theory and practice—and therefore must be repudiated.

Objectivity is a cognitive method that begins with direct observation of reality and proceeds to a higher level of intellectual understanding only by adherence to the fundamental principle of reality-based thought—the law of identity (or its corollary: the law of non-contradiction). At every stage of the process, facts, not whims—existence, not consciousness—set the terms.

But tragically, men are often non-objective, permitting other considerations to obstruct their commitment to existence. Fundamentally, all breaches of objectivity are primacy of consciousness manifestations in some form. They involve an individual placing some element of consciousness, e.g., his *desires* or the *beliefs* of others, above or before the facts. Examples of such an aberration abound. To consider only a few:

A child is raised by bigoted parents in a community where such prejudice against, say, blacks predominates. At school (or engaged in other activities) he has occasion to meet numerous members of the disfavored group and finds many to be of a high-minded moral character. But when he voices a dissenting opinion to the general view, he is met with vociferous disapprobation. Forced to choose between the facts that he has observed first-hand and the dominant belief of his community, he rejects reality and subscribes to the prejudicial viewpoint of the majority.

A second "everyday" example: today, early in the 21st century, an individual knows from many sources that heavy cigarette smoking is causally linked to serious heart and respiratory ailments. But he nevertheless chooses to begin smoking and, over the years, indulges his habit ever more frequently. He knows the probable long-term consequences, but he desires the tobacco—so he pushes aside facts, reality, truth in order to gratify his impulse, and concludes that somehow he will escape the fate that befalls others.

Third: an intelligent individual searches for moral guidance and embraces religion. His mind tells him that women are not turned to pillars of salt, that human beings do not live inside of whales, that men dead and buried in the ground are not revitalized, etc. But he pushes aside awareness of such disturbing facts and accepts on faith the religious beliefs he is taught. In general, faith is a cognitive method that starts with the teachings of a revealed text—the *Bible, Koran, Upanishads*, etc.—and accepts its claims unquestioningly. The believer *desires* the existence of a God who can accomplish miracles and grant him eternal life. Therefore, despite his intelligence and perpetually nagging questions, he dismisses all contradictory facts in favor of a set of beliefs that offer him solace, hope, and assuagement of his death anxiety.

A final example: on a grand intellectual scale, contemporary multiculturalists represent an *au courant* social version of the primacy of consciousness approach. Each individual is held to be no more than an inculcated drone of his society's fundamental beliefs, mores, and prejudices. He necessarily cognizes all events through the filter of the conceptualization he has socially imbibed. *He cannot escape the socially-derived conceptual filter.* Consequently, the beliefs of others, i.e., of society, are now intrinsically embedded in his mind as an unalterably dominant, subjective feature of cognition.

Any social version of the primacy of consciousness theory, including multiculturalism, codifies traditional conformity—the abject choice to surrender one's mind to the group—into a full-blown epistemological theory. *The theory upholds conformity in the absence of volition.* Individuals do not choose to reject an objective assessment of the facts. They are incapable of it. Men do not voluntarily select a primacy of consciousness method and abjure the primacy of existence approach; rather, as the multiculturalist conceives it, such an outcome is inescapably inherent to the process of their "socialization."

In fact, some individuals *do* succumb to the beliefs of their community and interpret observational facts and events through the prism of such a socially-absorbed intellectual framework. But this is a *choice* they make—not a necessary, automatic, non-volitional manifestation of society's cognitive dominance. Observe that many individuals, both historically and currently, make different choices, and repudiate the most fundamental beliefs of their families and/or their societies. For example: at least hundreds of thousands (and more likely millions) of human beings, raised in totalitarian states, indoctrinated with teachings of the superiority of Communism (or some other dictatorial ideology), and with hatred of the capitalist West, throw it off, independently develop a fierce longing for freedom, and risk their lives to escape to the Free World. Further, mankind's greatest heroes develop revolutionary theories and often stand alone against a society hostile to the new ideas (a truth dramatized vividly in *The Fountainhead*). Socrates, Copernicus, Galileo, Darwin, Pasteur (and Ayn Rand herself) are merely several illustrious examples of innovative freethinkers who rejected and significantly amended the intellectual framework of their respective societies.

It is important to grasp that multiculturalism, and the primacy of consciousness theory more broadly, necessarily deny not merely the metaphysical but also the epistemological aspect of objectivity. In philosophy—as well as in historic and contemporary influence—the two dominant primacy of consciousness manifestations are: religion and collectivism (i.e., the modern social school, including multiculturalism). It is instructive to contrast Ayn Rand's distinctive theory of cognition with both of these schools.

The religionists hold that knowledge is based in faith. Human beings need no active process of cognition; the mind passively accepts the teachings of a revealed text. In effect, the supernatural consciousness controlling existence simply imprints what it wants human beings to know on the impressionable and essentially inert "clay" composing their minds.

By contrast, the modern subjectivists of the social school claim that the mind is vigorously operative in the process of gaining knowledge; that it imposes its socially-absorbed principles on the raw data of sensory observation to construct the world known to man. Human beings are active cognitive agents, not passive receptacles of divinely-ordained commandments—but the very features they necessarily employ in cognition warp the raw data, cleaving men inexorably from knowledge of a metaphysically independent world.

Consequently, the epistemological alternatives offered mankind are: faith or subjectivity—knowledge of a "higher" world or no knowledge of this one—passive fantasy or active distortion. Both schools agree: self-initiated mental activity is not the means to knowledge. A cognitive method is either an unnecessary or a disqualifying element of cognition. Either the mind does nothing—and gains knowledge by "faith;" or it does something—and precludes itself from gaining knowledge. According to both schools, knowledge of an independent reality is not gained by application of a volitionally chosen and distinctively human method of cognition.

But, according to Ayn Rand, knowledge is of existence, of this independently existing world, not of a 'higher" fantasy realm; and is gained solely as a result of men's choice to employ an active, reality-based method of cognition. Both the religionists and the subjectivists are crucially wrong in epistemology: human beings do require an active cognitive method; passively awaiting revelation from an all-powerful cosmic consciousness will not avail men so much as an attenuated glimmer of knowledge. On the other hand, the human mind's systematic adherence to the rules it must follow to cognize reality is not a distorting mechanism, precluding its subsequent conclusions from the status of knowledge; rather, it is the indispensable factor making knowledge possible. Knowledge is not gained "no how;" nor does the "somehow" of a proper method—the method of logic—disqualify an idea or conclusion from the realm of objective truth. Following the method of logic is precisely what enables a human mind to reach objective truth—in any subject, including that of philosophy.

The conclusion is that a proper method of thought must be congruent with the two primaries of cognition: the facts of the independently-existing world and the nature of human consciousness. It must be based in the facts of reality, because consciousness does not possess primacy; it does not create, but rather can only perceive that which exists. It must be congruent with the actual nature of man's consciousness, because consciousness has identity—"the mind is not blank receptivity; it is a certain kind of integrating mechanism, and it must act accordingly."[11]

Therefore, we come to Ayn Rand's definition of objectivity, which captures the essence of the ideas developed in this chapter. "To be 'objective' in one's conceptual activities is volitionally to adhere to reality by following certain rules of method, a method based on facts *and* appropriate to man's form of cognition." By such means alone, man is rational and an efficacious cognitive agent capable of guiding his life successfully.[12]

In conclusion, the principle of objectivity has now been explained in both its metaphysical and epistemological aspects—and, as a consequence of examining in greater detail the specific method of rational consciousness, The Lesson of Objectivism has been explicated at a deeper level.

It has been seen that man inhabits a universe where existence has primacy over consciousness and in which consequently the rational mind is his instrument of survival. But it still remains to understand man in greater detail. For example: Does reason function automatically and involuntarily, as instinct does in animals—or must a man choose to employ it? Related: Is an individual in control of his own actions and destiny, i.e., does he have free will? Can he rise to great heights of heroism by dedicating himself to an indefatigable pursuit of life-promoting goals? Can he remain undaunted in such a pursuit even if confronted by formidable opposition? Or is he inevitably a helpless creature, an anti-hero, dominated by forces beyond his control, be they divine, social, genetic or other? To develop a theory of human nature, all of these questions must be answered.

Chapter 7

Man the Hero

That reason is man's means of survival has profound impact on the life of each individual. Based on this fundamental truth, Ayn Rand looks at man and observes a being who can control his own life and destiny. She does not see a being helplessly buffeted by social forces, as do contemporary Behaviorists and Marxists. She does not see a creature doomed by fate or tragic flaws, as did Sophocles and Shakespeare. Nor does she see a being wracked by repressed urges and torn by inner psychological conflicts, as do Freud and his heirs. She does not observe what other thinkers have claimed to observe.

Ayn Rand looks at man and sees the possibility of towering heroism.

The main characters of her novels make this abundantly clear. Observe how each is distinctively etched as a variation on a central theme. Howard Roark, for example, is an architectural genius who struggles for years against a conservative society antagonistic to his revolutionary designs. Hank Rearden is a superbly productive industrialist and innovative thinker who develops a new metal alloy—Rearden Metal—that is as superior to steel as steel is to iron. Dagny Taggart is a brilliant engineer who expertly runs a transcontinental railroad, who recognizes the merits of Rearden Metal before anyone else, and who stands against virtually an entire society to rebuild her railroad with the new substance rather than with steel. John Galt is a towering intellect—an exalted scientist, inventor, philosopher, statesman—a man whose accomplishments are so prodigious he could be compared only to such real-life geniuses as Aristotle, Leonardo da Vinci, and Isaac Newton.

Ayn Rand's view of man's nature in one word is that he is a *thinker*.

He is a being whose nature requires him to live by his own judgment, to never allow others dominance in his life, to neither conform nor rebel but to use his own mind. This, we have seen, is The Lesson of Objectivism: the mind is man's tool of survival and the deepest core of his nature.

But the mind does not function automatically.

Man is a being who must choose to be rational. This is what Ayn Rand means when she describes man as "a being of volitional consciousness." He must choose reason, he must choose reality, he must choose to live and function as man.[1]

Human beings have *free will*.

On Ayn Rand's distinctive theory, to say men have free will is to claim that they possess the power of choice, the capacity to govern the outcome of their own lives by means of the choices they make and the actions they perform based on them. It is to state that men are in charge of their own destinies, that they can select life-promoting values, enact the cause(s) requisite to achieve them, and thereby attain success and happiness. To a significant degree—despite such uncontrollable factors as physical make-up, the choices of others, and more—men can make their lives turn out the way they want.

Put negatively, to possess free will means that there is no external power controlling a man's life, no outside agency necessitating its result. Over the centuries, numerous thinkers, known as *determinists*, have argued that man is a helpless puppet, controlled by a higher power, be it God or Satan or Fate—or today, in a more scientific era, by his genetic coding, "environmental conditioning" or "socialization." To support free will is to argue that determinism, in any and all of its variants, is false.

On Ayn Rand's view, a man can achieve, survive and prosper on earth because his survival instrument is under his direct, volitional, individual control.

The most fundamental choice possessed by human beings is: to think or not. Thinking does not occur automatically. It is not like sensory perception. For example, when the wind blows or the sun shines brightly, a man feels it on his skin whether he chooses to or not. Similarly, the noise of a car in the street or a television in the next room is heard involuntarily, with no special act of focus required on an individual's part.

But reasoning requires a volitional act, a turning on of the cognitive apparatus, a process of focusing the mind. For example, an entrepreneur does not involuntarily, automatically think about the problems of production his firm faces; he must choose to do so. In any given moment, he is free to evade his responsibilities and turn off the mental switch. Similarly, a college student must voluntarily initiate his research and studying; he must choose to enter the library, open his books and concentrate on their meaning; in any moment, he is able to turn the mind off and let his studies lapse.

> To think is an act of choice...Reason does not work automatically; thinking is not a mechanical process; the connections of logic are not made by instinct. The function of your stomach, lungs or heart is automatic; the function of your mind is not. In any hour and issue of your life, you are free to think or to evade that effort. But you are not free to escape from your nature, from the fact that *reason* is your means of survival—so that for *you*, who are a human being, the question "to be or not to be" is the question "to think or not to think."[2]

Man, as Ayn Rand explains him, is a being of volitional consciousness. Knowledge of the existence of one's own free will is achieved by direct introspective awareness. An individual can direct his mental attention inward and observe himself in the very act of choosing. The college student, for example, may introspectively watch as he lets his mind wander to daydreams of his girlfriend, but then re-focuses it on his physics textbook. The application of one's mind is under one's own voluntary control—and the processes of powering the mind's attention levels up or down are directly apparent to an individual's examination of his own internal mental states.

Each individual makes his own choice(s)—and must continue to do so every day of his life. A man has the capacity to turn on his mental machinery and exercise his full powers of mind—or not. In every minute of his waking life, in regard to every issue, he must choose both the subject he thinks about and the degree of mental energy he expends. There is a continuum of effort; he may choose mental alertness, a state of unslackening readiness; or he may choose to let his mind drift passively, at the mercy of random stimuli or impulses of the moment; or he may work to turn off his mind, to turn it away from reality, to avoid facing some unpleasant fact(s).

For example, take the case of three philosophy students in a History of Modern Philosophy class. With an important final exam approaching, an exam that deals with the difficult theories of the philosophers Immanuel Kant and G.W.F. Hegel, they adopt contrasting strategies. One tackles the problem head-on—studying conscientiously, taking notes, bringing his questions to the professor, struggling diligently to master the material. A second student works sporadically, procrastinates until the night before the exam, then, working at home, allows his mind to wander from his notes to the stereo music in the background and back. A third student, failing the course, pushes it from his mind altogether, refusing to consider the painful topic, working to sever this issue from his awareness, to disintegrate his consciousness.

These are the three fundamental alternatives possible to human beings: full focus, drift, or evasion—or, put differently, active thought, passivity, or active avoidance—or, put differently again, face reality, float in and out, or flee from reality. The primary choice men have regards the manner in which they use their consciousness. Man's choice, fundamentally, is to reason to the conscientious best of his ability—or not.

This is the essence of volition. But based on this primary choice, individuals make subsidiary choices, as well. In terms of the previous example, the student who chose a full state of cognitive focus then selected a series of actions based on his fundamental choice. He chose to read, to take notes, to jot down questions, and to engage the professor in dialogue. The drifter and the evader, *qua* drift and evasion, make no secondary choices; they are confronted by alternatives only to the extent that they choose to face facts. But by choosing not to think, they inevitably bring on themselves harmful consequences: failure for the evader in this example, diminished success for the drifter. To the extent that a man chooses not to think, to that extent failure and misery inexorably follow in his life. .

It has already been established that rational thought is man's survival instrument. Therefore, in any set of circumstances, to suspend its use—to permit one's choices and actions to be driven by emotion or any other consideration—is to court failure, disaster, misery. The man who refuses to acknowledge that his chest pains could indicate a heart condition—or those who drive while intoxicated, ignoring the obvious risks—or users of toxic drugs, who choose to evade the consequences—or those who see aggressive enemies conquer their neighbors and/or bomb their cities but refuse to acknowledge that war is inescapably upon them—and countless others who wrest their minds away from terrifying or painful facts with which they do not wish to deal—are all examples of men who have put their lives inexorably in harm's way. The man who refuses to think is a man with an exceedingly short life expectancy.

There is no escape from either the responsibility or the consequences of choice in human life.

Man's survival and prosperity depend on the full exercise of his rationality, but man can (and often does) choose to act irrationally. Irrationality is a path to destruction, but man often—both historically and currently—chooses it. In brief, man can choose to abandon his mind, but he cannot do so with impunity.

> Man must obtain his knowledge and choose his actions by a process of thinking, which nature will not force him to perform. Man has the power to act as his own destroyer—and that is the way he has acted through most of his history.
>
> A living entity that regarded its means of survival as evil, would not survive. A plant that struggled to mangle its roots, a bird that fought to break its wing would not remain for long in the existence they affronted. But the history of man has been a struggle to deny and destroy his mind.[3]

A being who surrenders his tool of survival is helpless to deal with nature. Whether he then seeks survival by means of conformity, faith, feelings or force, he is unable to create the values his life requires.

The conformist, like Peter Keating in *The Fountainhead*, or an unprincipled politician ruled by public opinion polls, seeks truth by uncritically accepting the judgment of others; he is slavishly compliant to the group; his mind is surrendered to it, it dominates his existence.

The religionist, such as countless Jews, Christians or Muslims, seeks enlightenment in an imaginary supernatural realm; he believes in miracles, rejects reason for faith, and blindly follows the teachings of a revealed text and/or the pronouncements of the clergy.

The emotionalist, like many hedonists, pleasure seekers, and whim worshippers in our society, believes truth is created by his feelings, that if he feels it, it is true for him; he gives up rational thought and is driven by his urges.

The brute makes no pretense at being a man of reason; he seeks survival by criminal means, by initiating force or fraud against rational, productive men.

All of these types have relinquished their minds; it is not drug addicts, criminals, religious zealots or blind followers who create the knowledge, values, goods and services on which human life depends; survival for all of them depends on the productive activities of those who have not surrendered their minds.

Men often fail to be flawlessly consistent. They frequently hold and act upon mixed premises. For example, a real-life Peter Keating-style conformist, may, on occasion, choose to apply his mind to the issues of his education, his career, his love relationship. To the extent that he chooses rational thought his life is potentially one of success and happiness; to the extent that he eschews rational thought, choosing instead a policy of subordinating his judgment to the convictions of others, his life of self-betrayal leads inevitably to the empty misery of abandoned personal values.

Similarly, there are many "religious" men who are not predominantly—much less exclusively—religious. If a man consistently repudiates reason for revelation, and for example, chooses "faith healing" over medicine, his life expectancy is thereby severely diminished. But most "religious" individuals do not behave so irrationally. For example, they seek a secular education; they read books other than *The Bible*; they take scientific truth seriously, and often uphold evolution; they enjoy the modern advances made possible by man's mind; etc. Their religion and faith is actually a secondary component of a mixture that consists of premises grounded primarily in secularism and reason.

The explanatory principle of these and other examples is this: to the extent that men enact reason, their lives are potentially successful and fulfilled; to the extent that men reject reason, their lives are tormented, and, quite probably, significantly shortened. When human beings are consistently rational, they flourish. When they are mixed, the rational element of the mixture makes possible any degree of happiness they attain. When they are essentially irrational, their only chance of survival is as parasites off of rational men, e.g., conquerors or brigands—for such plunderers produce nothing; they merely pillage the values produced by the thinkers, until all are either already dead or faced with starvation.

Man's mind is the tool of survival even for those who repudiate it. In other words, human life depends on the choice to think, including for those men who choose not to do so, thereby defying their nature.

One important aspect of the principle of choice is: others can create an environment in which an individual is rewarded or punished for thinking—but they cannot themselves throw the mental switch to ignite an individual's thought processes (or to shut them off.) An individual can do that only for himself. "The mind is a terrible thing to waste," stated the beautiful slogan of the United Negro College Fund. An individual human being necessarily makes for himself the choice to waste or to develop his mind.

This point can be highlighted by remembering that some of history's greatest heroes were individuals *who chose to think under social conditions where it was dangerous to do so.*

Part of the point of *The Fountainhead* is that, tragically, mankind's greatest thinkers were generally rejected by society, and had to fight a desperate struggle against the very men who would most benefit from the new ideas. Galileo, for example, is only one of history's freethinkers who was rejected and tormented by the leading institutions of his culture. Giordano Bruno, it must be remembered, was burned at the stake by the same mentalities who, decades later, threatened Galileo with torture. Socrates was also executed for the uncompromising originality of his intellectual work.

Further, death and/or physical torture are by no means the only dangers faced by those whose thinking outstrips that of their peers. In France, for example, Voltaire and Diderot were each imprisoned by the *ancien regime* for the boldness of their thought—and D'Alembert intimidated into temporarily severing ties with the writing of the *Encyclopedie*. Social ostracism is also a penalty imposed on innovative minds. Darwin's ideas, for example, were (and still are) opposed by religious fundamentalists. Pasteur's germ theory was considered crazy, Fulton's steamboat labeled a "folly," skyscrapers, suspension bridges, and electricity feared as dangerous. But the independent thinkers refused to relent; they continued the battle to develop and spread their ideas—and, in time, they triumphed.[4]

These creators are the greatest heroes of the human race, and illustrate several important principles: man's heroic potential—and the nature of heroism.

Human beings can rise to extraordinary achievement because the instrument that enables them to confront the challenges involved in creating values—the mind—is under their direct, volitional, individual control. Socrates chose to face death rather than yield his conclusions. Galileo chose to publish his great work defending the heliocentric theory in astronomy, *Dialogue Concerning the Two Chief World Systems—Ptolemaic and Copernican*, even though he had been warned not to by Church authorities. Darwin chose to face calumny and the wrath of Christian fundamentalists rather than abandon his mind.

Nor must one be a genius to choose unswerving commitment to one's rational conclusions. So-called "ordinary men" have often risen to heights of moral grandeur by supporting what they know to be true or right against formidable opposition. For example: honest police officers have struggled incorruptibly not only against gangsters—but, at times, against graft within their own department. Some teachers have battled for phonics against school boards seeking to impose the disastrous "look-say" method of teaching reading, and others have fought for inclusion of evolution on the science curriculum—all struggling to further education and the mind. As a final illustration, the prisons of tyrants around the globe are filled with political prisoners, i.e., with those whose only "crime" was to think and speak out against the abuses of the regime. The choice to be committed to one's mind—and to truth—is not the exclusive prerogative of the genius.

Observe the logical progression of Ayn Rand's thought. The achievement of values makes possible man's survival. Man's rational faculty is the instrument by which he attains values. His rational faculty—his survival instrument—is under each individual's direct control. Therefore, the pursuit of values—the quest for a noble success—the ability to face and surmount daunting obstacles—the refusal to ever surrender the struggle—are all under a man's volitional control.

Heroism is the relentless employment of man's survival instrument—against any and all opposition—in the quest for the values that make human life possible.

In *The Fountainhead* and *Atlas Shrugged*, Ayn Rand provides vivid portraits of the heroic potential in man's nature. Howard Roark conceives fundamental new truths regarding architecture; he is opposed by virtually all of society, including the woman he loves across a period spanning decades; he must battle against entrenched beliefs, social institutions, and governmental prohibitions; yet, he remains unwavering in his dedication to his standards, and in the end he triumphs.

The heroes of *Atlas Shrugged* identify a vital principle of human existence—the right of a man to live for his own sake—and defend it against a collectivist society intent on enslaving the individual. They go on strike, fighting for the freedom of man's mind, and in the end, succeed in transfiguring the world.

Even in cases where a hero's conflict includes physicalistic action, as with criminal investigations or military operations, serious thought is involved. First: effective police work or military campaigns themselves require diligent application of the mind; such activities are not governed by mindlessly brute force. For example, competent law officers think regarding the identity of a perpetrator and the means of apprehending him; efficacious soldiers think about strategy and tactics. Further, law officers and the volunteer soldiers of a free country have chosen the right side of the ongoing struggle between good and evil. They need some understanding of virtue to make such a choice—and to gain that, they must think. Related, the police officers and military men of a free society, in varying forms, protect the rights of honest, productive men to freely employ their survival instrument in the quest for flourishing life. *Such men are heroes because their valorous deeds are performed in protection of the mind.*

Heroism, in any of its forms, involves a volitionally-chosen course of action in support of man's mind and his ability to attain values. The hero is loyal to the mind and its achievements against any and all foes.

Ayn Rand states that her philosophy holds "the concept of man as a heroic being." It is now possible to see why. The mind is the creator of all the values on which human life depends. A hero is an individual consistently loyal to the mind in all contexts, one who creates and/or defends the rational values required by man's life, and one who chooses to do so in the face of any form of opposition.

This point constitutes a re-statement of The Lesson in a new form: Man's potential for heroism lies in his capacity to choose unrelenting commitment to the mind and its works in the face of any obstacles and all alternatives.

This is the potential inherent in human nature. This could be any one of us.

One need not be a genius to achieve exalted moral stature. Most of us cannot match the intellectual achievements of a Newton, Shakespeare or the fictitious John Galt, but we can match their dedication to the unbreached use of the mind. We can use our own intelligence to the conscientious best of our ability, always seeking in all contexts to identify truth—to stand by it and to live in accordance with it. There is a function served in *The Fountainhead* by the character of Roark's trusted friend, the construction worker, Mike Donnigan—and in *Atlas Shrugged* by Dagny's conscientious assistant, Eddie Willers. Neither are the geniuses that Roark and Dagny are; both are individuals of more modest intelligence; but both consistently face facts, employ their minds to perform their scrupulous best, and never evade or deny ugly truths. Their moral stature equals that of the great heroes. The all-important field of morality, as we will see in detail in subsequent chapters, is open equally to all regardless of ability.

Related is the point that individuals will reach differing levels of success. For a variety of reasons, some will achieve at a higher level than others. For example, Henry Cameron fails to reach the level of success attained ultimately by Howard Roark—and in Edmond Rostand's great play, Cyrano de Bergerac dies without achieving any of his practical goals. As one real-life example, the astronaut, James Lovell, never fulfilled his years-long dream to walk on the moon—but he flew four times in space, journeyed twice to the moon, and commanded Apollo 13, the venture whose luckless fate merely set the stage for one of mankind's most glorious episodes of heroism. All three of the above individuals, fictitious as well as real, are heroes.

Some circumstances are not under a man's direct, volitional control. For example, he may be born with a physical ailment incurable by the medical science of his day—or he may be the victim of an accident, disease or natural disaster—or he might be thwarted by the mistaken or even irrational choices of others, etc. Because of such uncontrollable factors, a man need not necessarily reach his specific practical goals in order to be a hero. But his rational consciousness and moral character are subject to his command. Therefore, to reach the level of heroism, a man need not be undefeated in quest of the specific rational values he pursues; he need merely be undaunted.

It has been seen, in essence, that reason is man's survival instrument; that man must choose its use, i.e., that he possesses free will; that each man holds direct control of his means of survival; and that the individuals who choose consistently to exercise it are the greatest achievers or heroes of the human race.

That the mind's accomplishments are what is fundamentally responsible for man's survival and prosperity is clear. But does this mean that those achievements are morally good? Is the advancement of man's life on earth the essence of virtue and rectitude? Certainly, many thinkers disagree. Religious zealots, for example, believe man's life on earth is insignificant, even evil, a mere testing ground for the beyond, and that virtue resides not in successful living, but in renunciation of worldly values as a necessary means of entering heaven. Contemporary environmentalists also repudiate man's well-being and prosperity, arguing that nature has value in and of itself, and that the sacrifice of man's standard of living in order to "save the environment" is a significant virtue. Not all moralists hold that benefit to man's life is the standard of moral value.

What makes something good? What determines the nature of evil? Is it God's will? Is it the judgment of society? The wish or whim of each individual for himself? Or is right and wrong based on objective thought, on rationality—on some fundamental fact of reality? These questions of ethics or morality are the most important questions of human life. Based on what we've studied so far, we are now ready to understand Ayn Rand's distinctive answers to them.

Chapter 8

The Nature of the Good

In previous chapters, we have discussed several of Ayn Rand's distinctive contributions to moral theory, such as the virtue of egoism and the union of the moral and the practical. What explains her unique approach to moral questions? The answer is that she upholds a revolutionary standard for measuring good and evil—one based not on the will of God or on the dictates of society or on the whim of each individual, but on the facts of reality.

Ethics, we know, deals with questions of right and wrong, good and evil, what men should and should not do. The fundamental question is: what makes an action or an individual good or evil? Human beings need a criterion or yardstick by means of which to identify such qualities. For example, if a man held that working hard and supporting himself by honest effort is good, many human beings would doubtless agree. But what makes it good? Is it God's will—or society's judgment—or each individual's belief for himself? Alternatively, is there some immutable fact of reality, some law of nature that requires productive work of men?

The question involves the relationship between values and facts, between men's moral judgments and reality.

> Is the concept of *value*, of "good or evil" an arbitrary human invention, unrelated to, underived from and unsupported by any facts of reality—or is it based on a *metaphysical* fact, on an unalterable condition of man's existence?...Does an arbitrary convention, a mere custom, decree that man must guide his actions by a set of principles—or is there a fact of reality that demands it? Is ethics the province of *whims*: of personal emotions, social edicts and mystic revelations— or is it the province of *reason*?
>
> Is ethics a subjective luxury—or an *objective* necessity?[1]

The Scottish philosopher, David Hume, in a famous passage inquired if an "ought" proposition could be derived from an "is" proposition, i.e., if judgments of good and evil could be based on matters of fact—and answered with a resounding "no." In terms of the previous example, Hume's claim is that while he could observe an individual working long hours, receiving a paycheck, paying his bills, devising a budget, putting money in the bank as savings, etc.—he could not discern the "good" in this. Where is the "good?" he asked. I cannot directly observe it—cannot see or taste or touch it. If I cannot directly observe "the good," he held, then the good is not based in facts. Hume concluded that there is no identifiable relationship between facts and values. Value judgments are not based in the facts of reality—but in some other consideration.

In various forms, this has been a popular belief. In the history of moral philosophy, three schools of thought have dominated this question. All have repudiated a scientific, logical, fact-based approach.

One school is the religious theory, which claims that God's will is the standard of right and wrong. On this view, morality is based necessarily in religion. Conversely, in the absence of belief in, and commitment to God, there can be no ethics, no code of right and wrong to guide human life. In *The Brothers Karamazov*, for example, one of Dostoyevsky's characters posits the claim that in a world without God all things become permissible. No moral principles would exist, no restraint could be placed on licentious, whim-driven behavior, and life would degenerate into debauched and violent chaos. This is a widespread belief among religionists.

On this theory, anything commanded by God is good by virtue of His will alone. So if He chooses to flood the earth, killing untold numbers of human beings—or to slay thousands of Hebrews for the crime of worshipping a "golden calf"—or to permit Satan, on a bet, to torment the virtuous Job—then such actions are good because He chose them. This was the dominant theory of Dark Age Europe—and, today, of the Jihad-driven Islamists. At a deeper level, this school of ethics is based in the religious version of a primacy of consciousness metaphysics.

A second school is the social theory. This is the view that society's "collective judgment" is the standard of right and wrong. So, for example, if society judges that the Aryan race is superior, and other races inferior, then military conquest and bloody genocide are virtuous because society deems it right. Or if society judges the bourgeoisie or middle class to be enemies of the people, then their extermination is morally permissible.

This secularized version of the religious code holds that *vox populi, vox dei*—the voice of the people is the voice of God. It is the school of thought that underlies and gives rise to both National Socialist and Communist collectivism—the belief that society is all-powerful and that the individual must utterly subordinate himself to it—and is the dominant code of the modern Western world; for it is held even by many who reject totalitarianism. In America, for example, virtually any policy can be endorsed if it bears the magical insignia of serving the "public good." In theory, this means that the "will of the public" is the ruling criterion of moral virtue; that the good is whatever the majority declares. In metaphysical terms, this ethics follows from the social version of the primacy of consciousness error.

The final school is the personal theory, which asserts that an individual chooses for himself what is right or wrong for him. For example, an individual's own feelings tell him whether it is morally appropriate to use toxic drugs or not—to indulge in indiscriminate sex or not—to work productively or sponge parasitically off of others—even to commit violent crimes or not. If it feels good, do it, was the refrain of the 1960s hippie movement, giving perfect expression to the code claiming an individual's desires constitute the standard of right and wrong—for him. This forms the code of the drug user, the promiscuously sexual, the liar, the cheat, the thief, i.e., the hedonist or emotionalist of any variety—and it is also a popular code in the contemporary West. In terms of metaphysical theory, this is the ethics proceeding from the personal version of a primacy of consciousness approach.

Hume articulated the form in which the question has been generally asked. The majority of thinkers throughout history have answered that there is no positive relationship between values and facts. These philosophers argued that matters of right and wrong are decided by somebody's will or whim—be it God's, Society's, or the individual's; that the laws and facts of nature are irrelevant to the questions of good and evil.

But the problem can be looked at from a fresh perspective. Ayn Rand poses the question in a revolutionary form. She does not take the existence of values for granted, and then inquire whether they bear any relation to facts. She asks a more fundamental question: What in reality gives rise to the entire phenomenon of *valuing*?

Once the question is raised in this innovative manner, it points directly to the answer: it is only because living beings must attain certain ends in order to sustain their lives that the very phenomenon of valuing arises. For example, it is only because a lion needs meat, without which it will starve, that it stalks, kills, and devours its prey. The requirements of a lion's life make food a value to it.

A living being's values are those things that its nature requires for its survival. The lion has no capacity to choose that meat enhances, or germs harm, its life; these are facts of reality that can be neither altered nor denied. There is no choice for any living being regarding the requirements of its survival—no choice and no whim. This is solely a matter of hard, objective fact.

It is important to stress this causal relationship between the requirements of an organism's life and its values. A plant must gain the water, sunlight, and chemical nutrients that its nature requires. An animal must find food and shelter from the elements without which it will die. A human being must produce the material necessities of his survival, a creative activity requiring reason and knowledge. But in every case, the organism's nature—the factual requirements of its survival—is the source of its valuing. In no case, is will, whim, or caprice the source of values. "No choice is open to an organism in this issue: that which is required for its survival is determined by its *nature,* by the kind of entity it *is.*"[2]

Ayn Rand points out that life (and only life) is an end in itself, the sole phenomenon that is not a means to a further end. So, for example, living beings act or breathe or—in the case of humans—think in order to attain flourishing life; they do not attain flourishing life in order to reach some further goal. One eats a nutritious meal in order to support oneself toward a fulfilled and joyous life; one does not reach a fulfilled and joyous life in order to eat a nutritious meal. More broadly, Ayn Rand's point is not the truism that one must live in order to pursue values. Her point is a radically new one: that one pursues values in order to live. This includes such spiritual values as wisdom, friendship, love, etc., which so critically serve the purpose of fulfilled life.

The value of any particular goal, X, can be determined only by reference to an ultimate goal toward which X serves as a means. "An *ultimate* value is that final goal or end to which all lesser goals are the means—and it sets the standard by which all lesser goals are *evaluated*." It is logically impossible for a series of means to extend indefinitely without some final purpose toward which they strive. "It is only an ultimate goal, an *end in itself*, that makes the existence of values possible. Metaphysically, *life* is the only phenomenon that is an end in itself: a value gained and kept by a constant process of action." Consequently, any specific value—education, productive career, love, etc.—is such only because it serves the process of attaining (or sustaining) the ultimate goal of flourishing life.[3]

An important realization is that only living beings face a constant alternative of life or death. Inanimate matter changes its forms but it can be neither created nor destroyed; its existence is unconditional. So a rock may be ground to dust, the dust scattered in a stream, where it becomes sediment and, in time, exists as sand on the ocean floor. The rock's constituent elements have simply changed form.

But a living being can die. Oak trees, lions, and men must attain certain ends to sustain their lives. Failing to do this, the organisms perish. Their constituent elements remain but their *life* is gone. It is only this fundamental fact—that a living being must achieve certain goals in the face of a constant alternative of life and death—that makes valuing possible. In a world devoid of living beings, one containing only the barren expanse of inanimate matter—like the dark side of the moon—there would exist no possibility (and no necessity) of valuing.

Leonard Peikoff makes this point succinctly: "No one will ever show that a man being shot and the bullet piercing his body are metaphysically interchangeable entities, since both are 'merely collections of atoms in motion.' One 'collection' can *die*; the other cannot...a living organism, but not matter as such, is destructible. The one can *become* inanimate; the other already *is*."[4]

The phenomenon of valuing, Ayn Rand concludes, logically presupposes the existence of life. "It is only the concept of 'Life' that makes the concept of 'Value' possible. It is only to a living entity that things can be good or evil."[5]

It is because of this that life is the standard of value. Because values exist only to promote life, it follows that the requirements of life must be the yardstick or measuring rod by reference to which a candidate for value is judged: if X does not promote life, it is definitively eliminated from the realm of values. For example, it is only because an education or nutritious meal promotes a human being's life that these things are good; it is only because a dose of poison or a blow to the head harms life or destroys it that these things are bad. That which promotes the life of an organism is the good; that which harms or destroys it is the evil.

An important distinction must be noted between the value pursuit of human beings and that of other species. Whereas plants and animals are incapable of choice regarding that which they pursue—their values, in one form or another, are programmed into their nature—human beings must volitionally strive to gain life-promoting values.

Plants, for example, dig their roots into the soil and grow their leaves toward the sun by physical necessity; they are incapable of refusing to seek chemical nutrients, sunlight, or water; incapable of refusing to engage in the processes of growth, respiration, or photosynthesis; incapable of repudiating the values their lives require. Animals, similarly, seek the values necessary to sustain their lives by means of instinct; they stalk game or run from predators or migrate south by virtue of a rudimentary form of functioning inherently built into their consciousnesses. A bird has no capacity to repudiate flying, and a lion none to refuse the hunt, etc. Plants and animals seek life-promoting values automatically by virtue of a pre-programming hard-wired into their nature, with no capacity to reject the process and act as their own destroyer.

Man, on the other hand, must *choose* an actively pro-life policy. Nature requires him to gain values in order to sustain his life—but does not impel him to automatically pursue the values he needs. Rather, nature permits him to wreak his own destruction; it permits him to act as a suicidal creature. Men can choose, for example, between productive work and indolence, between independence and parasitism, between healthy living and toxic drugs, between life and death. Tragically, through most of history human beings have chosen life-destroying paths. One prominent, though by no means only, such path is the endlessly recurring (and eternally futile) choice to seek wealth by aggression, murder, conquest, plunder, and enslavement—all of which destroys wealth and slaughters value-creating men—rather than by production and peaceful trade.

> A plant has no choice of action; there are alternatives in the conditions it encounters, but there is no alternative in its function: it acts automatically to further its life, it cannot act for its own destruction.
>
> An animal is equipped for sustaining its life [by means of its senses]...In conditions where its knowledge proves inadequate, it dies. But as long as it lives, it acts on its knowledge with automatic safety and no power of choice, it is unable to ignore its own good, unable to decide to choose the evil and act as its own destroyer.
>
> Man has no automatic code of survival...An *instinct* of self-preservation is precisely what man does not possess...Man has the power to act as his own destroyer and this is the way he has acted through most of his history.[6]

Ayn Rand's momentous insight—that the factual requirements of survival are the source of valuing—is the indispensable identification that serves as the foundation of an ethics based in facts and reason, not in faith and feelings. "The standard of value of the Objectivist ethics—the standard by which one judges what is good or evil—is *man's life,* or: that which is required for man's survival *qua* man." Because rationality is man's fundamental means of survival, all that which promotes the life of a rational being is the good—and all that which is inimical to it is the evil.[7]

Something is good only because it objectively promotes man's life; evil if it harms it. Right and wrong are determined by reference to the facts of reality, not by reference to divine commandment, social belief, or individual desire. The facts of reality or, phrased alternatively, the laws of nature—not the will or whim of any conscious being—is the ultimate arbiter of moral evaluations. Ayn Rand's ethical theory follows logically and consistently from her primacy of existence principle in metaphysics.

Since the concept of "good" comes into existence only because a man must reach certain goals in order to sustain his life, it follows that the good is for him to reach those ends which in fact serve his ultimate goal. So men must grow crops and domesticate livestock. They must build houses, manufacture clothing, and develop medicines with which to cure diseases. They need to invent the automobile, the airplane, the electric light, the telephone, the personal computer, the Internet, and a thousand other life-enhancing devices. To protect the rights of the individual, they must establish a free society and formulate the principles embodied in the United States Constitution and the Bill of Rights. To preserve mental health, they must master the field of clinical psychology. To bring beauty and culture into their lives, men must develop literature, music, painting, and sculpture. The good, in short, is to achieve the things that sustain one's life, i.e., to achieve values.

Observe that the values required by *human* life include far more than the obvious ones of food, clothing, shelter, medicine, etc. For example, flourishing human life requires education—because the mind is man's survival instrument, and it must be trained. Fulfilled life requires advances in both theoretical and applied science—because for nature to yield a bounty of wealth, its laws must be comprehended and harnessed. Similarly, prospering human life requires progress in philosophy—because human beings need a fundamental understanding of reality, of knowledge, of man, of right and wrong, and of society in order to establish civilization. As a final example, human life requires art—because in order to work productively and indefatigably, men need the spiritual fuel and uplift that only great art can provide.

Neither the values necessitated by human life—nor the means of achieving them—are obvious. Much of Ayn Rand's intellectual work was dedicated to identifying and establishing man's proper values. For example, *The Fountainhead* examines such questions as: Is prestige a value? Is power over men's souls and lives? Is money a value—and, if so, where does it fall in a rational man's personal pantheon?

Related, what are the means by which human beings attain life-promoting values? Is honesty, indeed, the best policy—or is dishonesty effective? Is integrity a virtue—and can it promote success—or does practicality require elements of moral compromise, of selling one's soul, of hypocrisy? Is justice a virtue—or does mercy take precedence over it? Should a good man be proud or humble? These are sophisticated questions, the answers to which require a full ethical system (more of which will be provided in the next chapter).

But one fundamental point regarding such issues can be made here: the contrast between Ayn Rand's approach to ethics and that of the three historic schools outlined above. For religion, ethics necessarily consists of revelations—the ineffable attempt to divine the commands of an unearthly, supernatural deity. For the social school, ethics consists, in effect, of endless plebiscites and public opinion polls—an attempt to record the ever-changing preferences of the populace. (In practice, this impossibly unwieldy approach is replaced by the edicts of the dictators, who supposedly rule in the name of the people: witness Lenin's immortal line that "the masses must be driven to their salvation.") Finally, for the personal school, ethics consists of unadulterated whim worship—the emotionalist embracing of impulses, urges, and desires, of visceral feelings as a proper guide to action.

For Ayn Rand, however, ethics is a *science*, a rational discipline studying the factual requirements of human life on earth. Its purpose is to identify the laws of nature, including of human nature that must be obeyed in order to attain fulfilling human life.

So, for example, prestige—the acclaim of society—is all-important on the theory upholding social omnipotence; but, on the reality-based moral code of Ayn Rand, prestige is of no value in the absence of personal worth—and even of little value in its presence. Similarly, power over men—or revelatory insight into the Creator's will—are values only on the premise that there exists an all-powerful God or society that one needs to rule or manipulate or threaten or cajole or ingratiate oneself with. But on Ayn Rand's fact-based theory, values reside fundamentally in the effective dealings with nature that permit men to achieve flourishing earthly life. Reality—not the whims of society, of individuals, or of fantasy beings—is the source of values.

Existence has primacy over consciousness—in ethics, as well as in metaphysics—in practical affairs, as well as in theory—in life, as well as in abstract philosophy.

The means of attaining values, i.e., the virtues, will be discussed in the next chapter. For now, two points suffice: that the questions regarding the nature of values, and of which actions or goals constitute the specific values of human life, are not easily answered—and that Ayn Rand's theory revolutionizes men's ability to identify those answers.

Ayn Rand's monumental breakthrough regarding the foundations of moral philosophy also provides a deeper understanding and validation of the principle of egoism, which was discussed earlier. Since only individual human beings live—indeed, at the deepest metaphysical level, only particulars or entities exist—it is important to understand that value achievement is a distinctively individual, personal pursuit. Each one of us, in order to survive and prosper, must attain the values our nature requires. A basic principle of a rational ethics is that just as life is an end in itself, so every living human being is an end in himself, not the means to the ends or welfare of others.

In *The Fountainhead*, Howard Roark makes the important point that just as there is no collective stomach to digest food, so there is no collective brain to think. Digesting, thinking, and the other processes of body and mind are distinctively individualistic activities. Similarly, there is no collective "life form" to seek values. Living—and consequently, both the possibility and necessity of value pursuit—is a uniquely individualistic function. Therefore, "man must live for his own sake, neither sacrificing himself to others nor sacrificing others to himself. To live for his own sake means that *the achievement of his own happiness is man's highest moral purpose.*" Life is the *standard* of moral value, but his own happiness must be the *purpose* of each man's life.[8]

That the requirements of life serve as the standard of moral value also helps deepen and clarify another important point: the congruence of the moral and the practical. Since values exist solely to promote life, a proper moral code is one that guides human beings to successful, prospering, joyous life. In other words, the exclusive function of morality is to enable men to achieve practicality, i.e., the practical success of achieving life. If a moral code is, in fact, impractical, then, by virtue of that alone, it is immoral, e.g., the code of self-sacrifice. If men cannot live by it, it is wrong; if they can only die by it, it is evil; if it cannot be successfully practiced, it cannot be good. By the nature and requirements of life, there can be no possible dichotomy between the moral and the practical. The two are, in fact, the same point—looked at from distinct perspectives.

Since rationality is mankind's survival instrument, the fundamental means by which values are attained and life made possible, it is man's primary virtue. Virtues are principles of action that are necessary for the creation of values, i.e., for the attainment of flourishing life. What other principles are indispensable to support human life? What are the virtues according to Objectivism? This is the next question to be addressed.

Chapter 9

Virtue as a Requirement of Survival

Because of religion's historical dominance in the field of ethics, virtue has generally been considered an ethereal quality too "fine" for this world. Based on this view, various monks and saints throughout the ages have sworn vows of poverty and chastity and proceeded to withdraw from active pursuit of values, holding that intimate involvement with worldly things sullied their moral character.

In reality, nothing could be further from the truth. Since the values upon which human life depends must be created by men's effort, the states of character which enable them to do so are sanctified by that alone. Virtues are first and foremost principles of action that, when integrated into a person's thinking, emotions, and behavior, become character traits. Such principles of action enable men to achieve values and live. Since values and all concepts of right and wrong come into existence only to support human life, character states are virtuous to the extent (and only to the extent) that they effectually advance that goal.

It has already been seen that rational thought is the fundamental means by which human beings survive and prosper on earth. Rationality is, therefore, man's cardinal virtue. But there are aspects of rationality that help to explicate it, derivative virtues that are expressions of the fundamental one. Ayn Rand identified six of these related virtues—independence, integrity, honesty, justice, productiveness, and pride—as a minimum of the characteristics required to lead a moral existence. These can be studied individually, but, in practice, virtue forms an indivisible whole. It is impossible to "practice any one of them consistently while defaulting on the others."[1]

Independence

Ayn Rand wrote that independence is "forming one's own judgments and...

living by the work of one's own mind." Howard Roark in *The Fountainhead* is an outstanding example. His architectural designs are original creations, neither copies of previous buildings nor obedient offerings to public taste. In his private life, he chooses his friends and his lover in accordance with his own standards and values—not to please his mother, Ellsworth Toohey, or society in general. In work and in relaxation, Roark's values and choices are guided by his own thinking.[2]

In real life, history's great innovative thinkers provide abundant examples of this virtue. Such men as Socrates, Galileo, Darwin and others stood up in support of ideas they knew to be true though it required them to stand alone. Usually, they received ostracism from their societies, at times even torture and death—but they persevered, refusing to betray their principles or their minds.

Nor does independence require genius. At a more prosaic level, a child who remains true to his career choice despite parental disapproval—or a teenager who refuses to use toxic drugs although it may bring upon him the scorn of his "friends"—or a politician who stands by his ideals despite their unpopularity with voters—are all examples of this virtue.

Observe that Roark and these other individuals are devoted to the full exercise of their minds; that, as with their other conclusions, they form their personal values and standards by acts of rational thought. In regard to moral issues, Ayn Rand holds that the good is a subcategory of the true; the good is simply the true applied to value questions; and, therefore, the identification of right and wrong in ethics requires the same scrupulous process of rational cognition as does the identification of truth in science (or in any other field). Both identification and evaluation demand independent thought.

An autonomous pursuit of truth requires a scrupulous devotion to the full application of one's own mind, a conscientious commitment to the process of thinking. "The term 'independent thought' is a redundancy." If an individual actively seeks new knowledge, checks the truth of all conclusions by reference to observational evidence, and integrates newly-grasped principles into the sum of his knowledge, then he is thinking. Nobody but the thinker himself can initiate or sustain this activity. Thinking, by its nature, is an independent function.[3]

A young child who avidly seeks to learn new facts and master new skills—who characteristically says "I can do it" and is characteristically eager to try—is a good example of nascent independence. Another example is a young man or woman of a Howard Roark type raised in a religious family. Such a person will question the dogmatic precepts of faith and struggle, perhaps painfully and haltingly, toward a fact-based, rational understanding. Similarly, an independent student, faced with a politically correct professor who aggressively pushes anticapitalist, anti-American views in class, does not passively submit to such brain-numbing indoctrination. To protect his grade, he may remain silent; but to protect his mind, he will critically examine the professor's claims, seek outside sources, study opposing theories, ask which school of thought accurately explains the facts, and reach his own conclusions.

Independence does not necessarily come at the cost of social rejection—the best, most rational members of society will practice, recognize, and praise this virtue. In real life and in a free country, as in Howard Roark's fictional story, independent men do not lack for those who understand, admire, and befriend them. Nevertheless, it is possible that the man who stands on the conscientious conclusions of his own mind will be ostracized by others. The independent man recognizes that social approval—*if it involves the surrender of his own mind*—is a mere Sirens' allure to self-destruction. Conversely, he understands that popular repudiation, though perhaps painful, is an insignificant price to pay for loyalty to his own rational conclusions and principles, i.e., loyalty to reality. At some level, he understands that existence holds primacy over consciousness, and that his life is furthered by honoring the facts, not necessarily the beliefs of others. To paraphrase Jesus in an Objectivist context and with an Objectivist meaning: what is the profit for a man to gain popular acclaim if he thereby surrenders his mind?

In this regard, it is well to remember the climactic words of Dr. Stockman in Ibsen's *An Enemy of the People*: "I am the most powerful man in the world—the man who stands alone." Stockman meant, and Objectivism upholds, the principle that a thinking individual—even if he must oppose all of society—is the most productive, efficacious, creatively unstoppable force amongst men. He embraces rationality—mankind's survival instrument—and thereby liberates himself from whatever ignorance, prejudice, and irrationality may dominate his specific society. When an independent man possesses genius, he is capable of positively transfiguring the world—as Galileo, Pasteur, and Ayn Rand herself, among others, have demonstrated. If he is of more modest intelligence, he is still capable of transfiguring his life.

Independence is remaining true to the most conscientious judgment of one's own mind, refusing to sacrifice it to the beliefs of others. Since a man's mind is his survival instrument, independence is a non-negotiable requirement of his survival.

The contrast with this is a state of dependency, of permitting others to dominate one's life. There are many forms of what Ayn Rand termed "second-handedness," the condition of parasitism on others. Peter Keating, Roark's foil in the novel, is an example of one of these varieties: conformity. In his youth, Keating held personal values: he had a budding interest in painting and, as a young man, loved Catherine Halsey. These two nascent passions, if permitted to flourish, could have filled his life with meaning and purpose. Tragically, however, Keating chose to betray the things and persons he loved. In order to please his mother, Ellsworth Toohey, and society, he surrendered his values, condemning himself to an empty, internally miserable subsistence.

Conformity is an uncritical acceptance of the ideas, standards, and values of others. It involves one form of placing others before self, of holding their judgment and thinking above one's own. The conformist surrenders more than his values to others; he betrays his judgment, i.e., the thinking by which he formed those values. The conformist surrenders his apprehension of reality to other men; in short, he relinquishes his mind. Keating perfectly expressed the meaning of this toadying mentality. "Always be what people want you to be," he said. In return for people's approval, the conformist is willing to hand over to them his judgment, his mind, and his soul.[4]

Real-life abounds with examples. The religious believer of any denomination who simply accepts the faith of his family—the cultist who unquestioningly obeys a Jim Jones-type leader—the aggressive social climber who rises to the top of an organization by means of adroit political manipulation, i.e., not by means of superb work performance, but by currying favor with all superiors—the individual who blindly follows the unthinking prejudices of the community in which he's raised and discards his own judgment to become a mindless bigot—all of these, and many more, embody the principle of conformity.

Nor is conformity the sole means of surrendering one's mind to others. The non-conformist is equally guilty of this vice, albeit in a different form. Where the conformist curries favor with others, the non-conformist derides the values of others and seeks to wound them. In effect, the conformist's concern is to discover the principles or ideals of others in order to adopt them; the non-conformist's concern is to similarly discover such principles and ideals—in order to scorn and repudiate them. Neither the conformist nor the non-conformist permits his own understanding of reality to serve as the cognitive compass or guiding element of his life. In both cases, the principles of other men—whether to embrace or reject them—are the ruling consideration. The beliefs of other people come first—to accept or attack. One's own mind is subordinated to others, who are thereby granted pre-eminent stature in one's life.

In *The Fountainhead,* the avant-garde writer, Lois Cook, is an excellent example of the non-conformist mentality. She cultivates a studied slovenliness of personal appearance and explains to Keating why she desires the ugliest house in New York. "They all work so hard and struggle and suffer, trying to achieve beauty, trying to surpass one another in beauty...Let's throw their sweat in their faces. Let's destroy them at one stroke...Let's be ugly." Her desire to "throw their sweat in their faces" is the hallmark of a non-conformist. Non-conformity is an uncritical rejection of the standards, the judgment, the values of others. As such, this cognitive policy is a form of surrendering one's mind to others.[5]

Independence means living by the work of one's own mind—not surviving as a parasite off of the work of others. In *The Fountainhead,* for example, Howard Roark performs original work, whereas Peter Keating sponges off of Roark's achievements and those of previous designers. Gail Wynand creates a journalistic empire by means of his genius and productive energy—Ellsworth Toohey, who creates nothing, seeks to take it over. In real life, honest men survive by creating the goods and services required by man's life, but criminals, welfare bums, and other deadbeats eschew such independent thought and effort and seek survival as leeches off of the producers.

The independent man retains control of his life—but the parasite, in a multitude of ways, is utterly dependent on others.

Given that the mind is mankind's survival instrument, surrendering it to others can only put a man's survival in peril.

Integrity

Ayn Rand wrote: "Integrity does not consist of loyalty to one's subjective whims, but of loyalty to rational principles." A man of integrity must hold rational principles—and he must remain true to them in action. "Man is an indivisible entity," Ayn Rand held, who "may permit no breach between body and mind, between action and thought..."[6]

To have integrity, one must: first, hold rational, i.e., reality-based, life-promoting principles. Unfortunately, many human beings, perhaps the majority, hold no firm convictions; their beliefs regarding intellectual issues, personal morality, the principles of a proper government, etc., are often vague generalities they absorbed from their families, religious training, or schooling. They neither think carefully regarding such issues nor form their own considered judgments.

By contrast, the man of integrity is a thinker: he is not content to uncritically swallow what other people believe—regardless of a person's importance in his life. He examines all claims by reference to observed facts and reasoned argument based on those facts. Like Howard Roark, he forms his own judgments. Virtue, as indicated above, is an indivisible whole; to practice one virtue consistently is *ipso facto* (by the very nature of the case) to enact them all. The man of integrity is necessarily independent.

Further, such an individual's practice is unswervingly congruent with his convictions. He recognizes that the ideals, the principles, the values he cherishes are not "mere abstractions" to be disregarded in practical living; rather, they must animate his daily life. He lives in undeviating accordance with the ideas he holds most dear—and knows that to betray these vital products of his thinking is to commit spiritual (and perhaps physical) suicide. He will never surrender the life-promoting convictions and values that provide meaning to his life.

Examples abound in the kind of heroes extolled by Howard Roark in his climactic courtroom address. Such creative geniuses as Robert Fulton—inventor of the steamboat; John Roebling—designer of perfected suspension bridges, including the Brooklyn Bridge; William Lebaron Jenney and Louis Sullivan—builders of the first skyscrapers—frequently met stiff opposition to their revolutionary ideas. But convinced of the superb value of their advances, they refused to compromise their progressive visions; they held their ground, stuck to their ideals, and, in the end, triumphed over all opposition.

This virtue can be illustrated as effectively on a prosaic as on a grand scale. Consider the life of a young man who chooses to be a writer. Such a choice is rational, i.e., it is entirely consonant with the educational and intellectual requirements of man's life. Nevertheless, the aspiring writer will, in many cases, face a daunting series of obstacles. His parents, for instance, recognizing the financial difficulties of such a career, may disapprove, urging him to study medicine rather than literature. He studies hard to gain an outstanding education in his field—but, in numerous instances, must overcome the irrational ideas and inept teaching of his professors. After college, he struggles to learn his craft and earn a living—but though he must wash dishes to make money, and for years papers his walls with editors' rejection slips, he perseveres, never relents, and in the end, achieves a significant literary success.

To carry through on rational ideals, on life-promoting values that make life possible and meaningful—never betraying them no matter the roadblocks or travail—is to have integrity.

Ayn Rand does not hold that a difficult struggle is inherent in a virtuous man's quest for value achievement and happiness. He will work diligently and effectively; the most rational men will recognize and honor that; and his life path through education, career, and personal relationships need not be fraught with rejection, hardship, or pain. But the story of Howard Roark dramatizes the point that *even if the quest for self-fulfillment is blocked by imposing obstacles*, the man of integrity—and only such a man—will still triumph. Ayn Rand's code is simultaneously a realistic and inspirational explanation of the indispensable role of integrity in the pursuit of personal happiness.

On Ayn Rand's theory, there is no other way to attain practical success. To be successful is to achieve rational, life-promoting goals. But to do this, one must first hold rational, life-promoting goals—and, second, one must pursue them dauntlessly, never surrendering or betraying them. This is the virtue of integrity. The Howard Roarks of the world—whether geniuses or not—will succeed; the Peter Keatings of the world—regardless of their brains or talent—will fail.

The cliché on this point is that a man should practice what he preaches. But this is true only if, in fact, what he "preaches" constitutes rational principles and values; for then *the only way* to success and happiness is through practice of them.

There exists a sharp contrast between the Objectivist conception of this virtue and the conventional account. Generally, integrity is held to be the "practice what you preach" virtue—regardless of what you preach. On this view, one can be a Nazi, preaching and practicing genocide, but as long as one is not a hypocrite—so long as one refuses to betray one's principles in action—one possesses integrity.

In Ayn Rand's thinking, such a conception represents a profound error. Virtue exists solely to achieve values and thereby promote life. *There is no virtue in allegiance to death-dealing principles.* Like Hitler, one can support a code upholding tyranny and murder; one can suffer and die fighting for it—but virtue is not the result. On the contrary, unwavering loyalty to murderous principles only certifies one as among the evilest men of history. Ironically, the only way to mitigate such evil is precisely by refusing to practice the vicious principles one endorses, i.e., by a policy that would be conventionally labeled "hypocrisy."

The deeper reason that devotion to life-destroying principles lacks any shred of virtue is that all such ideas, and the actions based on them, are irrational, i.e., are at war with reality and embraced only by evasion. Here, the Nazi example can be continued. The Nazis claimed inherent moral superiority based on bloodlines, i.e., on inherited racial or *biological* characteristics. Unfortunately for them, the entire science of genetics refutes such a claim, showing that moral characteristics are neither based on nor transmitted by men's bodily chemistry.

But to the Nazis, reality was considered a minor annoyance. Their solution was simply to deny the unpleasant truth, push aside the facts clashing with their beliefs, and rewrite the biology textbooks to suit their prejudices. Based on such Nazi "science," they justified their conquest and extermination of the "inferior" races.

Since the values necessary to promote human life must be achieved in reality—and since character states are virtues only because they make such value achievement possible—no virtue is attainable by denying or evading reality. Death, destruction, and misery—in a multitude of forms—are the inevitable and necessary outcomes of such evasions. Where values are extirpated and life slaughtered, there can be no virtue of any kind, neither integrity nor any other.

Honesty

Ayn Rand wrote: "One must never attempt to fake reality in any manner." She stated that "the unreal is unreal and can have no value"—and made the revolutionary claim that "neither love nor fame nor cash is a value if obtained by fraud." Such an assertion is startling to many, who believe, for example, that a man can lavish stolen money on himself to the immense betterment of his life.[7]

Ayn Rand shows such a belief to be false. The achievement of the values necessary to support human life requires a scrupulous devotion to what is, i.e., to facts, to reality. Values cannot be created by concocting delusional schemes or fantasy alternatives to reality. Rationality—a conscientious allegiance to reality—is mankind's survival instrument. To build bridges, skyscrapers, or cities; to grow crops and domesticate livestock; to cure diseases; to invent computers and the Internet—to promote man's life in any form requires just such an unswerving devotion to facts. The honest man recognizes that reality exists—and only reality exists. Honesty, to state the point negatively, is the rejection of unreality.[8]

It is the very foundation of value creation that a dishonest man abrogates. A dishonest man weaves a network of lies that clashes with reality at every turn—then is stuck attempting to achieve values and live in this fantasy world. Such a task is impossible and he becomes a victim of the unreality he fabricated.

The virtuous man recognizes that just as truth is not to be gained by evading or denying reality, so no other value is to be gained by such a method. For example, wealth (the goods and services a man's life requires) can be created only by productive effort, not by fraud or deception. Physical fitness and long-term health can be maintained only by means of proper nutrition, exercise, and rest, not by an attempt to deny the body's nature or requirements. Self-respect can be gained only by means of rational achievement, not by a Peter Keating-like attempt to delude others into believing one has attained such achievements. The love of an honest man or woman is won (and kept) only by a life of scrupulous devotion to moral principle, not by foisting on him/her a pack of lies. The virtuous man understands, at least implicitly, that human beings have a nature, that flourishing life requires adherence to that nature, and that reality's laws cannot be flouted with impunity.

The most honest men know (or at least sense, feel or implicitly grasp) that dishonesty is not a means to the achievement of values—but to its opposite: to loss, defeat, self-destruction, death. At a commonsense level, many parents have grasped this point and taught their children: "Honesty is the best policy." Indeed, it is—and it is important to illustrate this principle in the realm of practical action. Leonard Peikoff makes the point in the following way.

Why, the question goes, should a man not perpetrate a brilliant fraud, bilking unsuspecting investors of copious quantities of unearned loot, and then escape to a foreign land, free to revel in his ill-gotten gains? Why not, indeed?[9]

Let us illustrate the question, draw out its logical results, and identify the ultimate and inevitable outcome. A consummate con man, let us say, sells vast amounts of stock in a phony company supposedly manufacturing a new kind of widget. He falsifies research data, forges documents of incorporation, counterfeits a detailed business plan, and swindles millions of dollars from unsuspecting "marks."

Such a course commits the confidence man to a (literally) endless series of lies. He lies regarding the research, the company's existence, the business plan, the prospect of future earnings. He lies to his investors when he sells his scheme, to his banker when he deposits his cash, to his acquaintances when he tells them what he does, etc. He lies regarding his background, his credentials, his plans, his final goal and destination.

Each falsehood he tells contradicts the actual facts of the case, rendering the con man susceptible to exposure by any acquaintance who knows any part of the truth. If a given individual knows anything about widgets, for example, or about the current research in that field or about the specific industry involved or about the con man himself—about his identity, background, method of operation, etc.—then he becomes a danger to be met with further lies. Further, what befalls if the scam is "successful"—if he is not apprehended but escapes to distant shores to enjoy his loot? When the money runs out or he misses the thrill of the crime or he is merely bored—the "success" of his initial spree prompts him to undertake a new such endeavor involving a new pack of lies.[10]

The details of a dishonest life will vary from case to case. But what remains constant is that reality is a unity—and that no part of it can be sundered from the rest and treated in isolation. All facts are interconnected, one leading logically to the next, and then to the next, etc. A dishonest assertion diverges from the facts at its inception and, in principle, is impossible to be self-contained. The con man, who doesn't work, when asked must claim that he does; if pressed further, must create the name of an employer, dates employed, etc.—a new set of lies—to cover the first. When a background check reveals he never worked there, it is answered with more lies. And so on.

Observe the necessary effects of such a course. One virtue the liar immediately relinquishes is independence. The dishonest man does not seek survival by means of rational cognition and productive work—but, rather, through the manipulation of others. "*People* become to him more real than the fragments of reality he still recognizes." The capacity to deceive others—not to understand (and create values in) reality—is his preferred method of seeking survival.[11]

Further, the dishonest man is not merely a dependent but, worse, a parasite on others insofar as they can be fooled, gulled, conned. He is utterly dependent on their ignorance, on their lack of knowledge, judgment, and insight. The more discernment, understanding, and penetration possessed by an individual—the more of a threat he poses. It is not merely the beliefs and expectations of others—rather than facts—that dominate his life; but their *false* beliefs, their—thanks to him—deceived, deluded, never-to-be-fulfilled expectations. The liar believes he has mastered others, turning them into his unwitting dupes; the deeper truth, however, is that he is now a servant of their misconceived hopes, catering to their delusions, fanning their futile aspirations, consigning his existence to the propping of their groundless anticipations. Ayn Rand terms such a man a fool—"a fool whose source of values is the fools he succeeds in fooling..."[12]

Virtue is a unified whole; to breach any aspect of it is to violate all aspects. Can a dishonest man have integrity? He either holds no rational principles—or he consistently betrays them in action. Can he be just? The con man (and liars generally) seek the unearned by deceiving and manipulating others, that is, by means of perpetrating injustice. Can he be productive? To the extent that he is dishonest, he seeks values by fraud, not by production. Is he rational? His attempts at survival are based on unreality, not reality. (See below for discussion of justice and productiveness.)

This is the fatal, not-to-be-escaped flaw in the liar's scheme. It is possible to deceive some men, at least in the short run. But how does one deceive reality? The most "brilliant" lies will not serve to grow food, cure diseases, build homes or office buildings, mass produce clothing, invent the electric light or the automobile, airplane, personal computer, Internet, etc. The liar depends on honest men to create the values his life requires. Without their productive efforts, he cannot survive. If they adopt his dishonest methods, then all men starve or freeze or die of disease. The liar's methods cannot achieve values, cannot sustain prosperous life. They lead only to the squandering or destruction of values. *Human beings survive only by rational achievement, not by dishonesty.* If most men are honest, then a few parasites might briefly survive by leeching off of their productive effort. If most (or all) men are dishonest, then they quickly perish together.

To ask whether it is in a man's rational self-interest to attempt survival by dishonest means is to ask: Is it beneficial to his long-term goals to make unreality more important than reality—to surrender his ability to attain independent survival—to require victims—to make all honest men a threat to him—to turn their rationality, intelligence, and insightfulness into his gravest danger—to pit himself against reality and its representatives, rational men—to live on the run—to hide, lie, fake, answer exposure with more lies—to exist in chronic fear of retribution and guilt at the realization that such is all one deserves—to sink deeper into the morass of unreality—to end with apprehension or an inability to distinguish truth from delusion or with both—is such a subterranean existence in his rational self-interest? Why—when by contrast a shining world of values can be created by rational effort?

Here is the deeper meaning of Ayn Rand's claim that neither love nor fame nor cash is a value if obtained by fraud: values, the requirements of life, must be created by human effort; such creation requires specific states of character. Values, the effect, cannot be attained by abrogating virtue, the cause. Values sustain life—and cannot be achieved by means destructive of life. *Nothing can be a value if it involves the surrender of a man's rationality.* With what faculty could he then hope to sustain his survival? To nullify man's means of survival is to nullify the possibility of it. Irrational men can "achieve" violence, destruction, and miserable penury; but joyously fulfilled life is perennially beyond their capacities.

Justice

Ayn Rand provides a concise explanation of justice in *Atlas Shrugged.* "Justice is the recognition of the fact that you cannot fake the character of men as you cannot fake the character of nature, that you must judge all men as conscientiously as you judge inanimate objects, with the same respect for truth...that every man must be judged for what he *is* and treated accordingly..."[13]

Justice involves two components: men must be judged strictly by reference to the facts of their actions, with the judge(s) blind to all other considerations—and those actions must be evaluated by a rational standard of right and wrong, i.e., by the standard of man's life. Justice requires that human beings reward those individuals whose actions objectively promote man's life—and punish those whose actions harm it. Men's characters are not equal—and their moral choices vary widely. Heroes, for example, are not to be treated similarly to criminals. "In essence, justice is the policy of preserving those who preserve life. It is allegiance to those who have sworn allegiance to life." In brief, justice involves a rigorous rationality in the assessment of human beings, oneself as well as others.[14]

Since justice is rationality in the evaluation of men, its practice necessarily begins (continues and ends) with the most stringent devotion to facts of which a man is capable. In all cases, not merely criminal ones, justice must be blind to all other considerations but the objective truth. Even in a case potentially involving negative truths regarding a man's spouse, his child, his country, or anybody (or anything) else he loves (or holds dear and holy), a just man is unstinting in his quest to identify the facts. He recognizes that facts are facts; that they do not change merely because he wishes them otherwise; and that his sole opportunity to ameliorate painful situations lies in facing them for what they are.

But facts provide data or the raw material of understanding; of themselves they do not yield the knowledge necessary to guide men's lives. To do so, they must be appraised by reference to a rational standard of value—and that, of course, is the standard of man's life. Justice requires asking of any individual, event or quality: is it (or him) in keeping with the survival requirements of mankind—or is it inimical to them?

Take several illustrations from the field of politics: Thomas Jefferson, George Washington, Benjamin Franklin, et.al., fought for liberty against the British monarchy; they established history's freest nation; they risked their "lives, their fortunes, and their sacred honor" for the cause of individual rights and limited government. At the opposite end of the political spectrum, men like Adolf Hitler, Josef Stalin, and Mao Tse-tung struggled to establish totalitarian states; they unleashed terror on both their own citizens and foreigners—and murdered tens of millions of innocent victims. Under their blood-drenched regimes, no one had any rights; all were slaves of the state. All of these men (except Franklin) were heads of state; but their principles, their policies, and their programs could not have been more divergent. These are the facts, which must first be scrupulously identified. But what is their proper evaluation?

The founders of a free nation, by protecting the right of each individual to pursue his own values, immensely furthered the cause of human well-being and happiness—and deserve veneration, undying respect, and emulation; men around the globe should seek to replicate their principles and practices in their own countries. On the other hand, the founders of totalitarian regimes, by murdering millions and enslaving many more, furthered only the related causes of death, destruction, and misery. Consequently, they deserve nothing but men's utmost scorn and opprobrium; indeed, they deserve nothing but execution.

An important principle of justice is the *necessity* to pronounce moral judgment—*by reference solely to the facts of each specific case and in accordance with human life as the standard of value.* Ayn Rand reverses Jesus' exhortation to "judge not, that ye be not judged," and states that men must "*judge, and be prepared to be judged.*"[15]

The need for such a policy follows logically from Objectivism's ethical fundamentals. Men have free will—and can make rational choices or irrational ones. They can choose, for example, between principled honesty and chronic lying, productive effort and parasitical survival, supporting freedom or totalitarianism, etc. Men's rational choices promote life; their irrational ones harm it. To pronounce moral judgment is to reward the life-giving—to praise, support, uphold it in every form; and, simultaneously, to condemn the death-dealing. Such a policy is to support life and punish those who negate it. It is to be conscientiously rational in the judgment of men, i.e., to recognize the facts of their character, to assess such facts by reference to an appropriate standard, and to act accordingly.

Since the actions of rational men support life and those of irrational men harm it, the blunt truth is that one's very survival depends on distinguishing between the good and evil among men, on identifying each for what it is—and on supporting the former and opposing the latter. Honoring and upholding the principles of Thomas Jefferson—and denouncing and opposing those of Mao Tse-tung—literally made a life-and-death difference to millions of human beings. Justice, as with all moral principles, is a virtue because men's survival depends on it.

Further, it should be pointed out that men must judge themselves in accordance with the same rational standard they employ to judge others. If a man makes an honest error, for example, he must identify it and work assiduously to correct it. If he commits a moral breach, he must openly acknowledge it, make restitution—where possible—to any and all innocent victims, and strive to conscientiously reform his character. If he attains a significant achievement, he must honor himself and experience pride. A man's actions either enhance life or sabotage it, his own first and fundamentally—therefore, in service of his own survival and well-being, he must be conscientiously just in assessing his actions and character.

Additionally, Ayn Rand made the significant point that though it is vital to condemn and punish the wicked, it is of far greater importance to reward and celebrate the good. This is because the good is fundamentally the rational—those individuals who recognize reality and thereby promote life. The good is far more powerful than evil, i.e., it alone is capable of dealing efficaciously with reality and achieving values. The evil is impotent because it is the irrational, the reality-defying or evading. Consequently, it is capable of only destruction; it cannot create.

The first mandate of justice is to identify, reward, defend, and preserve those who are good. "Evil must be combated, but then it is to be brushed aside. What counts in life are the men who support life. They are the men who struggle unremittingly, often heroically, to achieve values. They are the Atlases whom mankind needs desperately..." and such Atlases need to know that they live in human societies that value the individuals and the actions that promote life.[16]

The criminal who robs innocent victims must be apprehended and punished—but it is far more important that the industrialist who produces wealth be esteemed and honored. The tyrant must be overthrown, condemned, executed—but it is of vastly greater significance that the founders of the world's freest republics be venerated. Though the liar must be admonished, the honest man is of the first moment; he, before reckoning with the devious, must be duly commended. Justice, first and foremost, involves applauding and rewarding those who make possible prospering life.

Several widely-held moral theories clash with the virtue of justice. One is the principle of mercy, which is defined as: unearned forgiveness. Mercy applies only to the evil and stipulates an undeserved condonance of its transgressions. Good men seek justice, not mercy; they ask only what they deserve or have coming to them. But the wicked seek to escape their due requital; they desire to inflict harm and avoid proper retaliation. Many moral codes endorse mercy, but Christianity takes especial delight in this flagrant abrogation of justice. By refusing to appropriately punish evil, this principle fails to deter it, thereby emboldening it to ever greater atrocities, and thereby inevitably harming the good. The moral creed of mercy, in essence, offers up the good as a sacrifice to the evil.

Even worse, however, is the modernist code of egalitarianism. This is the theory that urges the eradication of justice and the imposing of an attitude of universal moral equality. The theory holds that "equality supersedes justice." To be blunt, if all men deserve equal evaluation and treatment, then there exist no moral distinctions between Thomas Jefferson and Adolf Hitler. According to egalitarianism, "the most heroic creator on earth, the most abysmal villain, and every person in between, should share equally in every value, from love to prestige to money to important jobs...regardless of what any individual deserves or earns..." Egalitarianism represents a full collapse from a rational code of assessing men's moral character; it offers a blank check to evil. If no moral distinctions hold, then no disapprobation or punishment can redound to the commission of even the most heinous crimes. More important, no pride or praise should properly result from the performance of the most heroically life-supporting deeds.[17]

Egalitarianism is the most vilely consistent annulment of justice ever proposed—but injustice in any of its incarnations has but one inescapable result: the abandonment of the good to the unrestrained depredations of the evil.

Productiveness

Ayn Rand wrote that "productive work is the process by which man's mind sustains his life, the process that sets man free of the necessity to adjust himself to his background...and gives him the power to adjust his background to himself."[18]

Productivity consists of the actions required to create the values upon which human life depends. Since man is a composite of mind and body, production of the knowledge and material wealth necessitated by human life requires both intellectual and bodily work. Productivity is the application of human understanding to the physical creation of the goods and services men need to sustain their lives. Such mind-body integration is true whether the productive act consists of measuring, sawing, and hammering nails into wood to build a chair or table—or designing and constructing a skyscraper—or writing a novel or physics textbook—or one of a thousand other creative acts. All productive work involves constructing, building, creating, growing, nurturing, or bringing into existence something that did not previously exist—and something (a good or a service) that is beneficial to human life. In all cases, this involves both mental and physical effort.

That human survival depends on productivity should be readily apparent. Every value required by man's life—from crops to computers, from apartment buildings to antibiotics—must be created by human effort. Although the higher animals find ready-made in nature the necessities of their lives—whether grass, berries, caves or other creatures on which to prey—human beings cannot sustain themselves in such fashion. They need houses, not burrows or caves; medicines to cure disease; telephones and the Internet for urgent communication; cars and jet travel for comfortable transportation; and a thousand other values, all of which need to be invented, discovered, cultivated, produced.

Human beings do not and cannot adapt to their environment. They cannot grow thicker fur in winter and shed it in summer; they do not migrate with the seasons—or hibernate; they can not shelter under rocks or in the branches of trees. Because it is not their nature to passively accommodate themselves to their milieu, they are not at the mercy of environmental conditions. Ayn Rand pointed out: "If a drought strikes them, animals perish—man builds irrigation canals; if a flood strikes them, animals perish—man builds dams..." and similarly if blizzards strike them, animals freeze—but men build homes and heat them with gas, oil or electricity. By constructive achievement, human beings adjust their natural surroundings to themselves.[19]

Since that which furthers man's life is the good, the production of the values on which human life depends is the essence of a moral existence. Paraphrasing Howard Roark, values must be created before they can be given away. It is the production of values, not their charitable distribution to others that is the virtuous, i.e., the life-giving act. The great productive geniuses of history—e.g., Andrew Carnegie, John D. Rockefeller, J.P. Morgan, Bill Gates—are the truly virtuous individuals; not a "saint" of charity like Mother Theresa. The great producers create the goods and services upon which human life depends; the saint of charity—at best—convinces productive men to voluntarily support the needy; at worst, seeks to inculcate guilt in the producers for their "selfish" lives, and/or to besmirch their names because of their great wealth, and/or to promote governmental initiation of force to impose a welfare state on the producers.

A legitimate goodwill towards one's fellow man—kindly acts motivated by value, not self-sacrifice, performed joyously, not dutifully, such as those of Dagny to Cheryl in *Atlas Shrugged*—is logically posterior to productiveness. Benevolence is a subsidiary issue in ethics, because human survival does not depend on it. An individual's life requires him to produce either the goods on which his survival depends—or their value equivalents, to be exchanged for such goods; sharing his produce with his fellow man is optional.

But whereas kindly goodwill, expressed always to the innocent, never to the guilty, is a legitimate aspect of man's life, fully congruent with virtue, the vice of self-sacrifice never is. Self-sacrifice is a logical antipode to all virtue, to virtue as such, including to productiveness. Virtues are the character states required to achieve values—but a self-sacrifice code demands that man relinquish them. The productive individual creates the values upon which his life depends; the self-sacrificing man surrenders them. The code of producing values makes man's life possible; the code of betraying or yielding them makes it impossible. Productivity is the code of flourishing life; self-sacrifice is the code of death. In the life of an individual, productiveness leads to higher living standards and increased happiness; self-sacrifice, to betrayed values, exacerbated poverty, and diminished joy. In the life of a society, productiveness is an integral component of capitalism and widespread wealth; the self-sacrifice code inherent in collectivist dictatorships is the cause of enslavement, forced servitude to the state, and grinding penury.

The fundamental means by which productivity is achieved must be understood. Manual labor certainly provides a legitimate contribution to the productive process, but contrary to Marx and the materialist school of philosophy, it is not fundamental. Ayn Rand established in *Atlas Shrugged*, as discussed above, that man's mind is responsible for the creation of every idea or device that advances his life on earth. "Every form of material asset beyond an animal's level, beyond wild fruit or raw meat eaten in a dank cave, is made possible by man's cognitive faculty: by intelligence, imagination, ingenuity." Knowledge and reasoning ability are "necessary to make a Stone Age club, let alone the tools and weapons of the Iron Age"—never mind the computers, medical cures, agricultural technology, skyscrapers, jet travel, electric light and appliances, etc., of the 21st century.[20]

The enormous, life-giving productivity of the current era was made possible by the Scientific, Technological, and Industrial Revolutions that began during the Renaissance and the Age of Reason—and that accelerated during the 18th century Enlightenment and the centuries following. The underlying social condition that made possible the intellectual progress of the modern Western world was the identification of the principles of individual rights and limited government. The causation was reciprocal: increasing commitment to reason led to the realization that human beings must be free to guide their lives by their own minds—and increasing political-economic freedom led to enormous intellectual-scientific-technological advance.

After the Scientific, Technological, and Industrial Revolutions, it should be clear that the mind is the fundamental cause of man's material prosperity. After *Atlas Shrugged,* it should be clear that such production of wealth represents a profound moral virtue. It follows from this last point that the so-called "Robber Barons" were not larcenous blackguards to be vilified—but, rather, productive geniuses to be gratefully celebrated. Such industrialists as Andrew Carnegie, John D. Rockefeller, J.P. Morgan, et. al., and their contemporary counterparts, solved the problem of material production that had plagued mankind for millennia. These men and others like them created prodigious quantities of inexpensive steel, oil, automobiles, computers, medicines, etc., that fueled building and achievement of every kind, enabling the men of the free countries to attain standards of living that were historically unprecedented. Given that productiveness is a significant moral virtue, justice behooves men of goodwill everywhere to thankfully acknowledge the enormous contributions to their material lives wrought by these great producers.

Pride

Ayn Rand explained "that as man must produce the physical values he needs to sustain his life, so he must acquire the values of character that make his life worth sustaining—that as man is a being of self-made wealth, so he is a being of self-made soul."[21]

According to Objectivism, pride is more than the inner experience of a high self-esteem; it is an intellectual and physical commitment to one's own moral perfection—a recognition that such is possible and a refusal to settle for less.

Moral perfection requires neither infallibility nor omniscience. Human beings make honest errors, and as long as they work to learn from and correct them no moral flaw is implied. Moral perfection, by contrast, involves an *unbreached rationality,* a commitment to reality and thought, a repudiation of the irrational. An individual who understands this is unfailingly benevolent toward honest mistakes (both his own and others) but unremittingly intolerant of moral violations (again, both his own and others). He categorically abjures the policy of evasion. "He does not demand of himself the impossible, but he does demand every ounce of the possible." The essence of pride, Ayn Rand holds, is the quality of "moral ambitiousness."[22]

As some individuals work unsparingly for the value of physical fitness, as some study assiduously to gain an education, so the proud man strives to attain

moral perfection. He knows that a man's character is his most priceless posses-
sion, that no object or reward can be a value if it involves violating the sanctity
of his character. The proud individual understands that his life depends on an
uncompromising devotion to rationality; so that his dedication to moral perfection, his refusal to sanction or remotely tolerate moral blemishes, is of life-and-
death concern. Assessments of oneself as good or evil, right or wrong, worthy of
esteem or scorn are made by application of a sole standard: one's "volitional use
or misuse of [one's] tool of survival."[23]

On these premises, such a man will enact two related policies: he will never
shirk responsibility for his actions—and he will never accept undeserved guilt
for them. When he lives consistently in accordance with life-promoting principles, he achieves his values, his happiness, and a high degree of self-esteem. If
he ever violates those principles, he recognizes that the ensuing guilt is just. He
then renounces his wrongful behavior, re-thinks his premises, identifies and cor-
rects his error(s), makes restitution where possible to individuals unjustly
harmed, and thereafter conducts his life more rationally.

But on this same understanding—that the moral is the volitional, that a man
is fully responsible for every choice he makes and *only* the choices he makes—
he categorically repudiates guilt for any factor outside the range of his choice.
For example, he was not born in sin—he scorns the claim that he is guilty for his
birth. He accepts no turpitude for momentary desires on which he refuses to act.
He is not guilty for his race, his gender or his nationality—and is justly proud of
every penny of wealth, every measure of success, every ounce of happiness he
has earned by his own volitional rationality and effort.

The reward of a life devoted to moral perfection is an ennobled vision of
oneself, an exalted self-esteem. A man committed to the fullest use of his rational consciousness deals efficaciously with reality; therefore, he is self-
confident. Further, in practicing an inviolate rationality, in applying the principles of a life-supporting ethics to his own mind, life, and actions, he cultivates
an experience of profound self-worth. "Self-esteem is a fundamental, positive
moral appraisal of oneself—of the process by which one lives and of the person
one thereby creates." It is an amalgam of two conclusions, each of which a man
must earn: I am right and I am good—"I can achieve the best and I deserve the
best I can achieve"—I can live successfully and happily on this earth—and I am
worthy of it.[24]

Ayn Rand's position on pride stands out starkly because of the endless attacks made against this virtue by moralists across the centuries. Religion is a
primordial foe in this regard. Christianity, for example, damns pride as one of
"the seven deadly sins," and argues that "pride goeth before a fall." Humility—
the belief that man is sinful, that moral rectitude proceeds only from God, and
that man must abjectly seek His forgiveness—is hailed as virtue.

The doctrine of human sinfulness and imperfectability is obviously self-
fulfilling; for if men accept the claim that they are inherently vicious and incapable of independently attaining virtue, then they will not strive to live nobly.
Men are motivated to strenuous struggle by the ideal of the possible, not the
impossible. Believing oneself to be good is the basis of expecting oneself to be.

Similarly, though tragically, believing oneself to be evil is the basis of the opposite expectation. No individual who sincerely accepts the claim of his own sinfulness can ever be motivated to strive for virtue. Endlessly falling, he must either beg God for forgiveness, confess his sins, surrender his soul to the clergy for spiritual guidance—or overtly embrace evil and thereby serve as a cautionary tale the religionists can use to frighten their flocks.

As with many evils, the doctrine of individual worthlessness originated in religion and was then secularized by modern collectivism. The National Socialists and Communists, for example, regard an individual human being—his goals, his dreams, his personal values—as worthless. Only his unquestioning willingness to sacrifice for others, to selflessly serve a cause "higher" than himself, whether the race or the working class, enables an individual to acquire moral value. Hitler, it will be remembered, infamously stated: *"Du hist nichts, dein Volk ist alles"—"You are nothing, your race is everything."*

The moral principle should be clear. Just as pride is an integral component of an egoist ethics, its antipode is an integral component of an altruist one.

The attack on pride is a direct and logical result of altruism. Men who know their own worth will surrender neither their lives nor their minds to others, but will seek their own values in pursuit of their own happiness. Only individuals crippled by claims of sin and inherent guilt will so lack in self-esteem as to relinquish their own dreams and goals and turn their lives over to a "higher cause"—be it selfless service to the family or the state or God. The apostles of anti-pride are the apostles of power—seeking control over men's broken spirits, bodies or both.

It is logical that an altruist ethics has always served as the foundation of political authoritarianism. For if virtue is anti-egoistic, if it resides exclusively in selfless service to a "higher" cause, then what of those individuals too selfish to voluntarily practice it? The only answer consistent with such premises is that the state must be empowered to legally coerce such recalcitrant individuals to perform their duties, i.e., their unchosen moral obligations. Therefore the Dark Age Church, the contemporary Islamists, the National Socialists, the Communists are similarly adamant: men must kneel before the all-powerful ruler—religious or secular.

The simple truth is: proud men will refuse to obey. But individuals made to feel their own guilt or worthlessness will. Ellsworth Toohey makes the point in *The Fountainhead* that great men cannot be ruled—and that, therefore, it is undesirable to have great men. The historical attacks on pride represent a relentless and concerted attempt to convince human beings to surrender their lives and their minds to the purveyors of selflessness.

Many misguided individuals engage in sundry hapless attempts to boost their self-esteem. They try to impress others regarding purported accomplishments, they join "consciousness raising" pop-psychology groups, they seek people who offer reassurances that momentarily assuage their chronic anxiety. But reality is not to be cheated by second-handed means—and men are not to be talked into a value that can be gained only as a consequence of an undeviating allegiance to moral principles.

For example: what if a real-life Peter Keating-type succeeded in gaining extensive social adulation (as Keating himself does in Part One of *The Fountainhead*)? In and of itself, will widespread acclaim make him more honest? More independent? Will it enable him to live with more integrity? No. Winning many people's support will make one popular—not rational. It might provide a momentary jolt of emotional pleasure, like a drug; it might temporarily stave off awareness of one's moral failings, and the desperate insecurity that is its necessary emotional consequent. But it is woefully insufficient to make somebody willing, ready, and able to face reality and achieve life-promoting values. This is the problem for such a second-hander; for it is only that exact willingness to face reality that enables a man to attain any value, pride or another. To gain an effect, one must enact the requisite cause. To attain an incomparably elevated self-esteem, one must live by means of an unbreached rationality, i.e., a life dedicated to moral perfection.

Conclusion

Now it can be understood that every virtue of the Objectivist ethics is an application in a specific context of the fundamental virtue of rationality. Independence is living by one's own *mind*, not sacrificing it to the beliefs or whims of others. Integrity is devotion in action to *rational* principles and values, not · merely to any random (or blatantly life-destroying) principles that a man may hold. Honesty is a rejection of the unreal, i.e., of the *irrational*. Justice is the judging of men in accordance with the *facts* of their actions and by reference to a *rational* standard of value. Productiveness is the exploitation of nature to achieve men's values—a process made possible fundamentally by man's *mind*. Pride is a life dedicated to the attainment of moral perfection, i.e., a life of uncompromising *rationality*.

This is why virtue is a unified whole of which it is inherently impossible to practice merely a part. If an individual is uncompromisingly rational, then he is *ipso facto* practicing all of the virtues.

Here again, in a new form, is The Lesson: Regarding every fundamental issue and question of human life, Objectivism is the philosophical system consistently and proudly upholding the glory and life-giving efficacy of man's mind. The specific theme of this chapter is that virtue is an inescapable necessity of man's survival. To make this point in a different form: unswerving dedication to rationality in all forms and contexts is necessary for a being whose survival instrument is the mind.

Since survival depends on virtuous living, does it follow that success and happiness similarly depend on a life of virtue? The conventional view is that only unscrupulous individuals claw their way to the top—and that principled men are doomed to defeat because they are too noble for this world. For example, observe the popularity of the cynical expression, "Nice guys finish last." What is the actual relationship between virtue and success—between the moral and the practical? This is the next question to be examined. We have already seen that Ayn Rand upheld congruence between them. Now we have sufficient information to understand the deeper reasons for it.

Chapter 10

The Moral And The Practical

The relationship between the moral and the practical has been a subject of study by philosophers for centuries. Unfortunately, the code of self-sacrifice, whether religious or secular, has been historically dominant, wreaking untold havoc in men's lives, including on this issue.

If self-sacrifice is the criterion of virtue, then the achievement of values is immoral, i.e., "selfish" in the conventional usage of that term; only their surrender to satisfy others is moral. Since, in fact, the attainment of fulfillment requires the achievement of one's values, a selfless code, dutifully lived out, leads necessarily to misery; only the selfish course leads to success. For example, if a man passionately desires a career in music, but is confronted by a family adamant that he surrender that path to instead practice medicine, he is presented with a dilemma: satisfy either himself or important others. The first alternative leads to value achievement and fulfillment—but is condemned as selfish; the other is praised as virtuous—but leads to value abandonment and misery. The consequence is the monstrously-inverted belief that immorality leads to personal gain and morality to personal loss.

On the code espousing self-sacrifice, each individual confronts a constant alternative. The choice is between: selfless virtue and selfish vice; goodness and gain; impractical idealism and "practical," unscrupulous realism; a life too "fine" or principled for worldly success and one committed to an unprincipled success. "In other words, commit yourself to virtues *or* to values—to causes *or* to effects—to ethics *or* to life."[1]

After the chapter on virtue, it should be clear that Objectivism categorically repudiates such a view. A code of moral principles is required to achieve flourishing life. A choice or path is moral *because* it leads to life, and *only* because it does. The rejection of moral virtue—a "life" of irrational vice—necessitates a miserable existence of failure, frustration, and untimely death. The conventional view upholds the claim that morality and practicality, virtue and success stand in inverse proportion to each other. The more consistently a man pursues one, the more surely he sunders his affiliation with the other. In contrast, *Objectivism maintains that these crucial principles stand in direct proportion to each other.* This does not mean that a moral man is guaranteed success; it means that his only chance to gain success lies in a life of virtue properly conceived.

Since human beings are neither omniscient nor infallible, nothing can unfailingly guarantee success to a man. He can commit innocent errors of knowledge, he may encounter human accidents or natural disasters, he may be thwarted by the errors or irrationalities of other men. All of these factors and more may be responsible for denying a moral man the practical goals he seeks.

Nevertheless, virtue is the sole path to enduring practical success. According to Objectivism, a moral man is a rational man—one who seeks to expand his knowledge, who flinches from no truths, painful or otherwise, who permits no division between his thought and his action, who is scrupulously honest, who is diligently and indefatigably productive, and who persists relentlessly in courses of action he knows are right. The moral man, as the consistent employer of man's survival instrument, is the individual preeminently capable of attaining survival. To gain any desired effect, the requisite cause(s) must be enacted. Virtue is to value achievement what causes are to effects.

One consequence of Objectivism's fundamentals is the theory—startling to many—proclaiming the impotence of evil. There are two related points to be understood. The first is that evil is incapable of creating values; the second, that it is capable only of destroying them.

The evil is the irrational, the evasive, the anti-mind-and-thinking approach to life. It denies reality, eschews facts, rejects truths unpalatable to it. By placing itself outside of reality, it inherently disqualifies itself from all capacity to deal efficaciously with reality. The chronic liar, for example, prefers a fantasy realm to the one that exists. The parasitical moocher seeks to leech off of others, rather than engage in productive work. The historic epitome of overt irrationalism, the Nazis, rejected the science of biology to murderously and self-destructively cling to their nightmare theory of genetically-inheritable characteristics of moral superiority.

But lying, cheating, mooching, evading, initiating force and/or any similar policy are incapable of creating values. Such "methods" cannot grow food, build cities or cure diseases, to name but a few life-giving achievements. They are as ineffectual a means of promoting human life as a child's temper tantrum, which they resemble, though with vastly less justification. To repudiate the mind is to relinquish man's sole means of achieving survival.

The inevitable consequence is that evil men cannot achieve independent life. Evil men are incapable of dealing positively or constructively with reality—they are *metaphysically impotent.* But an impotence of constructive ability does not necessitate a similar impotence of destructive ability. Indeed, the very paucity of creativity necessitates destructiveness—for how else could irrational men survive except as blood-suckers, in some form, on the men who produce values?

Therefore, human history becomes the tragic struggle between first-handers and second-handers dramatized in *The Fountainhead.* Family bums sponge off of their relatives; non-productive leeches seek handouts from the welfare state; criminals victimize honest men; dictators suck the blood from their own citizens and then initiate wars to conquer their neighbors. When a man who eschews reality still seeks survival, he necessarily transforms himself into a drain on, if not a menace to, the lives of rational men.

There are individuals of mixed premises, to be sure, who combine elements of rationality and irrationality, good and evil in their lives. But to the extent that such a man achieves values and lives, it is the rational element of his character responsible for it. To the extent that he abjures reason and reality, he condemns himself (and generally others) to a tortured (and brief) existence.

The emotional accompaniment of value achievement is: joy. For example, if an individual studies assiduously and graduates from college with honors—if he works diligently in a field about which he's passionate and gains a hard-earned promotion—if he honestly woos the woman he loves and wins her—the emotional result of reaching such goals is the experience of profound joy, what the French term: *joie de vivre*—the joy of living. Joy is the positive emotional state engendered by the achievement of a life-supporting value.

There is an unbroken causal chain connecting the vital principles of human existence: reason—values—success—joy. Rationality is the sole means of attaining values, and success thereat is the sole means to joyous living. Similarly, there is an unbroken chain of irrationality and loss. It is: unreason—value destruction—failure—misery. "He who evades renders himself impotent in action and thus experiences life as suffering."[2]

It must be emphasized that joyous living requires the achievement of *values*—those goods and goals that are rational, i.e., objectively life-promoting. Joy can not be reached by the attainment of goals that are irrational, i.e., life-harming or destroying. So the cheater, who temporarily avoids apprehension and punishment for his duplicity—the heavy drinker, who has not yet brought on himself serious illness—the Peter Keating-style status seeker who receives unearned prestige—are not examples of men living joyously. Theirs are goals men pursue in the absence of values; their attainment leads, at best, to a few momentary jolts of pleasure which, in the context of their lives, represent but momentary diminishments of the chronic anxiety, ennui or depression in which such miserable souls subsist. When such irrational pursuits are enacted as characteristic policies, then these individuals do not and cannot experience the radiant and unclouded joy of a rational value achiever. In the absence of changing their courses of action, these pathetic individuals decline, by their own choices, inevitably into the sump hole of misery and/or early death.

The attainment of life-harming goals is not the achievement of values. The temporary abatement of suffering is not the experience of joy. The irrationalist's momentary jolt of pleasure is but a pale analogue to a rational man's fulfilling sense of achievement and pride. Peter Keating's inner experience of reaching what he desires—prestige—is not Howard Roark's inner experience upon reaching what he desires—architectural achievement. Joy is the necessary resultant of the attainment of values—and only of the attainment of values.

Happiness, it must be pointed out, is a type of joy. In Ayn Rand's immortal formulation, happiness "is a state of non-contradictory joy…" It comes from the attainment of rational values in all arenas of an individual's existence *over the span of a lifetime*. Happiness is a consistently joyful inner mode achieved only by the most rigorous pursuit of values across the full breadth of a man's life. Indeed, happiness is a demanding state that few individuals actually achieve—but one that is, potentially, attainable by all.[3]

It is possible to examine the specific requirements of happiness. Notice that happiness involves a form of "non-contradictory" joy. This means that all of a man's pursuits are rational; that he is not a mixed case in which some of his goals are values and some of them anti-values, like the hard-working career person who simultaneously embezzles money or uses drugs or cheats on his wife. The productive work in a field that fascinates him will bring him income, pride, fulfillment, joy; the irrational activities will bring only guilt, anxiety, and such negative practical consequences as diminished health, and/or apprehension and termination, and/or the loss of his marriage, and/or numerous other sources of misery. The life-harming actions undermine the joy he gains by means of the life-promoting ones. His life is then a discordant mixture of clashing elements. An absolute requirement of happiness is to extirpate the discord—and ensure that the range of his enterprises constitutes a concordant blend of exclusively life-enhancing pursuits.

The best examples of such a life come from Ayn Rand's novels. Dagny Taggart in *Atlas Shrugged*, for example, lives in an unbroken chain of value pursuit. In college she studies engineering, the field she loves, and excels; in her teenage years, she begins working for the railroad, the career about which she is passionate; she starts at the bottom and works her way up the railroad's organizational ladder, learning the business of running a railroad from the ground up, mastering the requirements of each stage as she inevitably progresses. Romantically, she is drawn only to men of noble character and superlative achievement—such giants as Francisco d'Anconia, Hank Rearden, John Galt, with each of whom, at various stages of her life, she shares a profound love relationship. Her final choice, the man who will be her husband—John Galt—is a towering hero whom she deeply admires, as well as loves. The man she chooses does not merely share her most precious values—the mind and its achievements, including scientific progress, technological advance, and industrial development—but is the world's greatest practitioner of these. Similarly, her friends and colleagues are men of great integrity, who share her passion for productive work: Eddie Willers, Ken Danagger, Ellis Wyatt, et. al. In art and entertainment, she values the beautiful melodic compositions of the composer Richard Halley, and man-glorifying works in literature, painting, and sculpture. In every quadrant of her existence, without exception—from education to career to love to friendship to art—she passionately holds and indefatigably pursues values. This is the way, over the course of a lifetime, that an individual achieves a radiant state of happiness.

It is not that a happy person experiences joy all the time—or that he does not suffer. Because even the greatest men make honest errors—because men with whom a rational individual closely interacts may make errors, honest or otherwise—because there exist germs, natural disasters, etc.—it is always possible that a moral man will lose a significant value. The necessary result of this is pain. In *Atlas Shrugged*, for example, Dagny experiences suffering upon the closing of the John Galt Line. In *The Fountainhead,* the same is true for Howard Roark when the Stoddard Temple is torn down. In real life, the world's greatest men may lose their parents, their spouse, or their dearest friend, experiencing profound suffering as the result. But in *Atlas Shrugged*, John Galt summarizes to Dagny the essence of a rational man's attitude toward such events: "It's not that I don't suffer, it's that I know the unimportance of suffering."[4]

The proper response to value loss is: grief over the deprivation—and renewed pursuit of further values. A rational man never fails to fully mourn his loss—but likewise never forgets that the meaning of life is achievement. The value achievement in a rational man's life, if graphed, would not necessarily form a smooth line upward; there may be peaks and troughs; but the long-term trend line is relentlessly upward. Happiness, for a rational man, is his normal state.

Ayn Rand's theory of happiness contrasts sharply with the two conventional codes that dominate discussion of this issue in our society: religion and hedonism.

Religion, by glorifying a transcendent fantasy realm, necessarily devalues life in this one. The most consistent embodiments of this theory in the West were the Catholic saints of the Dark Ages, who believed that this world was "a vale of tears," a place of unrelieved suffering necessary to test one's faith in God's ultimate providence, ensuring thereby—if one passed the test—entry into Paradise, as in the Biblical tale of Job.

Happiness, therefore, is out of the question; morally, men are called to a life of duty, sacrifice, suffering. One monumentally significant example of the importance of suffering to religion is the life and death of Jesus. According to the Christians, their God came to earth for the sole purpose of being tortured and murdered in order to provide a path to salvation for the sinners who choose to accept his sacrifice. The example he thereby set his billions of worshipers is that excruciating agony and loss of one's life in service of morally delinquent men is the highest ethical ideal.

Perhaps the worst tragedy of human history is that this doctrine became accepted by numberless millions as the epitome of virtue and the highest aspiration of man. "To an Objectivist, the adoration of pain is literally unspeakable. Morally, there is nothing to say about it beyond noting that its cause is the worship of death." The veneration of Christ on the crucifix is an eloquent example of this truth.[5]

Hedonism, on the other hand, purports to uphold man's happiness (or at least pleasure) as a pricelessly important value. Its fatal problem, however, is that it relinquishes all objectivity in its understanding of the good. It holds that joy proceeds not by gaining rational, i.e., life-promoting values—but by gaining *any* goals. Pleasure or happiness is not merely the *purpose of life* to hedonists—

it is the *standard of value*. So X is good *because* it gives pleasure to a man (or a group of them).

If, for example, the drug addict gains momentary pleasure from a cocaine "high"—or a bank robber from unearned loot—or a Peter Keating-style conformist from social acceptance—or the Nazis by murder of their "racial enemies"—then such actions are good by definition for those individual(s).

But although happiness is the proper goal of a man's life, it is not in fact the standard determining value. Something is good, and able to lead to enduring, long-term happiness only insofar as it adheres to reality, to the factual requirements of man's life. That some arbitrary action or acquisition brings an individual temporary, short-term pleasure is insufficient to certify it as objectively life-promoting. As we have seen, it is possible that an action clashing with the requirements of man's life may bring a few short-run jolts of pleasure, although in fact it promotes pain and even death in the long run. Presumably, for example, a drug addict might derive several moments of pleasurable titillation before he collapses from an overdose.

Actions objectively harmful or lethal to human life are incapable of generating happiness. "One must choose values by reference not to a psychical state, but to an external fact: the requirements of man's life..." It is literally a matter of life-and-death that the pleasure seeker distinguish between rational values and irrational pursuits, that he employ a standard of value that is objective.[6]

The religionists say: the pursuit of worldly happiness is selfish, sinful, materialistic—give it up. The hedonists, on the other hand, state: pleasure and happiness are good, so pursue them guiltlessly—by any means that you choose. One school overtly renounces happiness for suffering; the other causes suffering by means of the misconceived doctrine of happiness it endorses. One school upholds faith-based misery; the other, whim-based misery disguised as pleasure. Both schools repudiate any *objective standard* of value, thereby rendering each powerless to promote fulfilling human life on earth. Pain and untimely death is all either can achieve—and such is all that either has ever achieved.[7]

Since irrationalism in some form—religious or secular—has dominated history for millennia, human tragedy (and its expectation) has been widely prevalent. For the lives of irrational men *are* tragic—at best. At worst, they also wreak destruction on the good. If irrationality is prevalent in society, then it is logical that men will anticipate tragedy as the normal, to-be-expected condition of human existence. Ayn Rand dubs such a tragic vision of man's life "the malevolent universe premise."

On this profoundly mistaken view, the world is perennially closed to fulfilling human aspirations, non-amenable to value achievement, inhospitable to the pursuit of happiness. A man holding this theory knows that happiness is possible—but regards it as an aberration, an incidental random occurrence, an anomaly. It is the rarest of exceptions, hardly the norm of human life.

According to Ayn Rand, the universe *is* closed to the attainment of fulfillment and happiness by irrational men. For example, the cheater subsists in dread of apprehension; the thief exists on the run, finally either incarcerated by the legal system or killed by other thugs; the religionists deliver Hell on earth, whether the Catholic Church during the Dark Ages or the Taliban in Afghanistan; the Nazis murder innocent millions and lead their own country into devastation; the Communists likewise murder innocent millions before collapsing under the unbearable weight of their own irrationality; etc. Values, and consequently happiness, cannot be achieved by the rejection of man's survival instrument. In one form or another, reality inevitably deals untimely death to men who forsake their means of life.

The malevolent universe premise provides an empirically accurate forecast for the lives of irrational men—but it is not a truthful explication of the actual relationship between man and metaphysical reality. According to Objectivism, the attainment of happiness is moral—and more: because the world is intelligible to the rational mind, it is open to the achievement of rational values. Consequently, happiness is not merely possible—it is natural, normal, the to-be-expected state of a moral man. Ayn Rand refers to this theory as the "benevolent universe principle".[8]

This does not mean that the universe cares about mankind; it is not a conscious being possessing thoughts or desires. The principle expresses the theory that rational beings, understanding and adhering to the laws of nature, can and will achieve their values. A man who adheres to reality can and will reach his goals in reality. *A rational being can achieve rational values, thereby gaining happiness.* A rational man recognizes that failure, though possible, is an exception in his life, not the norm. "The rule is success. The state of consciousness to be fought for *and expected* is happiness."

Examples in fiction include such Ayn Rand heroes as Howard Roark and Dagny Taggart. In real-life, such giants as Thomas Jefferson and Thomas Edison, et. al., had enormously fulfilling lives—and their careers brought untold value into the lives of numberless millions. On the everyday level, it is the conscientious thinker—regardless of his intelligence—who studies hard at school, is diligent in his career, is scrupulously honest and trustworthy in his relationships and, as a consequence, achieves life-supporting values and long-term happiness. In *The Fountainhead* and *Atlas Shrugged*, the lives of Mike Donnigan and Eddie Willers respectively dramatize the applicability of this principle to those who represent the best of "everyman." The benevolent universe premise means that reality is open to the attainment of happiness by rational men—and only by rational men.[9]

That virtuous men have the capacity to gain happiness is now clear. But the question must be raised: What social conditions are necessary to promote this end? Since men flourish most not alone on an island, but in human society where they can gain education, friendship, love, and a division-of-labor economy, a question naturally arises: what type of political-economic system facilitates men's ability to practice a virtuous life? Or: since virtue is the sole means by which to create the values upon which human life depends, which social system unleashes men's ability to create values? Or: what is the system that encourages and rewards man's instrument of value achievement, his rationality—and which system(s) make its implementation agonizingly difficult, even impossible? Or: since rational value achievement is the sole path to happiness, which social system recognizes, respects (and protects) men's ability to gain happiness?

Put simply: Which social system maximizes men's ability to practice virtue? Which system rewards their commitment to rationality? Which system enables them to attain values? These political questions are next to be answered.

Chapter 11

Individual Rights and Government

What has so far been established are five basic points. Put briefly: men's lives require them to attain values; reason is their means of doing so; the propensity to promote or harm their quest for values constitutes the criterion of good or evil; the unyielding creators of values are mankind's truest heroes; and the achievement of values over the course of a lifetime constitutes men's sole means of gaining happiness.

The next question is: which social system is consonant with these fundamental truths?

The question of political philosophy is: what type of society enables men to practice the principles of morality? In Objectivist terms, this means: what type of society protects an individual's ability to be rational, achieve values, and thereby live to the fullest? The answer is: a society that recognizes and upholds the principle of individual rights.

There is, Ayn Rand argued, in agreement with America's Founding Fathers, only one fundamental right: the right to life. Its primary subsidiaries are the rights to liberty, property, and the pursuit of happiness.[1]

Since life is the standard of value, it follows logically that a man has the moral right to take every action necessary to preserve his life. Since we do not inhabit a Garden of Eden, and the values required by life must be produced by human effort, each man has the moral right to engage in productive activity. Since the mind is man's tool of survival, it follows that each man has the right to employ that tool without restriction. Rationality is man's survival instrument; consequently, his moral right to life involves a right to live as a rational being, to perform all the activities that a rational being's survival requires.

To explicate this point in further detail: each individual has the right to think whatever he will—and to express his thinking, verbally or literarily, as he deems fit. He has the right to employ his intellectual (and bodily) effort to produce the values his life requires. He has the right to pursue education as far as

99

he wishes to go—and in whatever discipline he chooses; to read, view or listen to any intellectual content he considers appropriate; to select any productive line of work he prefers; to accept any productive employment, at any rate of salary, he can find; to move voluntarily to any geographic area in which the opportunities for education and productive work are available. He has a right to pursue any specific activity congruent with his education, his intellectual expression, the development of his skills, and his productive work. Fundamentally, the moral right to live as a rational being means the right to think—and to produce values.

Human society obviously is capable of conferring great benefit in service of a man's life. Education, friends, love, family, and a division-of-labor economy are merely several of the significant boons an individual may derive from others. But there are also potential hazards. Human society also may include violent criminals, political dictators, military conquerors, and other dangers to an individual's life. It is far safer for a man to live alone on an island than, for example, in Hitler's Germany or Stalin's Soviet Union, because at least on the deserted island he is free to deploy his mind and effort in pursuit of his survival. There are no evil men initiating brute force against him, seeking to plunder, enslave or murder him.

The right to life and its derivatives protect a man's ability to seek and gain values *in a social setting*. There is no need of such a concept or principle for a man living alone on the island. For there, nothing exists to prohibit him from taking action in service of his life—and nobody that needs to be restrained by recognition of his right to life. He is free on the island to employ his mind, ingenuity, and effort in an attempt to gain the values he requires. Storms, wild beasts, natural disasters, etc., though a danger to his survival, impose no restrictions on his freedom to employ his survival instrument. If he wishes to live, he can (and must) employ his rational faculty in the face of whatever he encounters in nature.

But other men, and only other men, can prohibit his life-promoting activities—and only by initiating physical force or fraud (an indirect use of force) against him. This means more than the obvious point that they can end his life by means of initiating lethal force. *Any* degree of initiated force, in principle, impedes a man's thought; specifically, it restricts or prohibits his ability to *act* on his thinking. For example, if brutes of any variety—religious fanatics, Nazis, Communists or mere common criminals—hold a gun (or a sword) to a man's head, they can force him to act in contradiction to his thinking, i.e., against his rational consent. Although the brute cannot insinuate his hands inside the victim's mind and literally change his thinking—he can render the victim's thinking irrelevant to his action. He can physically restrain the victim from acting on his rational conclusions. Any initiation of force against an innocent victim, no matter the degree, curtails his ability to apply his thought to productive, life-sustaining action. A human being restricted from employing his survival instrument is thereby undermined in his ability to survive.

To illustrate this critical point: left free, a man will choose to hold onto his money (or his home or his land or other valuables)—but under compulsion he surrenders it to a gunman. The victim realizes that if he is unable to retain the wealth he earns, then he cannot survive—reality will, in time, terminate his life; but if he does not hand over the wealth he's earned to the brute, his life will be terminated *now*. The force initiator interposes his weapon between the victim's understanding and autonomous choice—and his ability to act on that under-standing and choice. The victim is thereby placed in a hopeless position. As the hero of *Atlas Shrugged* states to all would-be force initiators: "Reality threatens man with death if he does not act on his rational judgment; you threaten him with death if he does. You place him in a world where the price of his life is the surrender of all the virtues required by life…"[2]

Even if the initiation of force does not entail the threat of imminent death—even, for example, if it involves merely the theft of a few dollars—it undermines a man's ability to employ his resources in support of his life. If he has no re-course against such theft, then he has no means of preventing his financial life blood from being drained. How then is he to exercise his right to life? The con-clusion is that the initiation of force always undercuts an individual's ability to employ his mind in support of his own existence. An absolute requirement of a civilized society is that it bans such actions violating men's moral right to seek survival as a rational being.

Because a man's survival depends on his freedom to employ his mind, he possesses the moral right to do so without restriction. Other men have no moral right to physically impede an individual's freedom to act on his own rational conclusions. To be comprehensive in this formulation: no man has the right, for whatever reason, to initiate force against any other man.

There is no other human evil that can prevent a man from thinking, creating values, or reaping the benefit of the values he has created. For if other men re-frain from initiating force in any and all of its manifestations, then the sole means they have of interacting with him is: persuasion. In that case, no matter the toxic irrationality of their doctrines or specific ideas, an innocent man is free to repudiate them and live a rationally productive existence. *Persuasion cannot harm a man without his voluntary consent.*

A "right," says Ayn Rand, "is a moral principle defining and sanctioning a man's freedom of action in a social context." Rights define an individual's prop-er relationship to others; rights lay down moral guidelines that must be observed by each and every individual (or group of individuals) in their interaction with each and every other individual (or group of them). Ayn Rand provides a bril-liant elucidation:

"Rights are a moral concept—the concept that provides a logical transition from the principles guiding an individual's actions to the principles guiding his relationship with others." This is the concept that preserves and protects the per-sonal morality of a man in a social milieu. The concept of rights is the connec-tion "between the moral code of a man and the legal code of a society, between ethics and politics. *Individual rights are the means of subordinating society to moral law.*"[3]

What follows is that if human beings agree to live in society, and thereby gain its potential benefits, each individual member—and society as a whole—

must begin by recognizing the moral requirements of human beings in a social setting. The parameters within which each individual holds unquestioned authority, in accordance with the laws of a life-promoting moral code, must be identified. Within these boundaries, each human being takes action without need of sanction from other individuals or from society as a whole; within such boundaries, no one may properly seek to physically restrain him.[4]

One critical aspect of a man's right to life is his right to the property that he earns by his own thought and effort. Human beings must create the material values upon which their physical survival depends. The right to property is the key moral principle recognizing and protecting men's ability to do so. As Ayn Rand explains this principle: men have "the right to gain, to keep, to use and dispose of material values."[5]

The validation of an individual's right to property is simple. For example, men need shelter, and to ensure their survival they use a portion of the money they earn to buy a home or rent an apartment. What would happen to them if they had no right to this process—if someone could seize their residence or the money with which they pay for it? Without a place to live, they could not go on living for long. The principle is identical regarding the clothes they wear, the food they eat, the automobile they drive to work, or any other value they seek: men's lives require that they have the right to any and all values earned by their own minds and effort. In the absence of the right to property, there can be no right to life.

Recent history provides a vivid contrast between societies in which the right to property was protected—and those in which it was repealed. In the United States, for example, despite many violations, the right to private property was and is largely recognized. Millions of hard-working individuals own their homes, their own land, their own farms, their own businesses, etc. Immigrants still flock to America from repressed nations all over the world, in part because here they can fulfill their dream of owning something that belongs exclusively to them—a land where the legal system will protect, not itself violate, that right. The result has been the most productive and wealthiest country of history.

In the former Soviet Union and other Communist states, by contrast, private property was abrogated, farmers were forced off their own land to live on collective farms, and millions who refused were cold-bloodedly murdered. Not surprisingly, the result of such moral abomination was economic collapse. The right to private property is an integral, inseparable aspect of an individual's right to life. A rational, reality-adhering philosophy is an integrated, comprehensive system. A moral-political principle such as "rights" therefore rests on the entire body of thought underlying and giving rise to it. The key point in this context is that a man's right to his life and its corollaries follows directly from the basis of ethics: that the requirements of life form the standard of moral value. The derivation is straightforward: the good is that which promotes human life—and the evil that which harms it. Only *individual* human beings live or can die; only an individual's life can be promoted or harmed. An individual's right to his life makes it possible for him to live. In the absence of such a moral principle, he cannot. Therefore, an individual's right to his life—and its corollary principles—are good without qualification. "If man is to live on earth, it is *right* for him to use his mind, it is *right* to act on his own free judgment, it is *right* to work for his values and to keep the product of his work. If life on earth is his purpose, he has a *right* to live as a rational being: nature forbids him the irrational. Any group, any gang, any nation that attempts to negate man's rights is *wrong*, which means: is evil, which means: is anti-life."[6]

It is important to emphasize that rights are moral principles that sanction a man's freedom of *action*. A man has the inalienable right to his life, to engage in the productive activities necessary to sustain his life, to employ his mind as the fundamental tool of doing so, and to be free of the initiation of force against him. In brief, he has the right to take action in support of his life—and therefore to the freedom of action necessary to do so.

He possesses no right to be kept alive at somebody else's expense. He has no right to another man's life, his mind, his work or the product of that work. If he did, it follows that the expropriated individual has no right to these things—that he could be plundered, enslaved, murdered by those who have a right to them. There is, Ayn Rand explains, no such thing as a right to violate someone's rights. (Because of this, any charitable help a man extends to his fellow men must be *voluntarily* undertaken. Aiding another person(s) is a choice a man makes, not an unchosen obligation imposed on him as a necessary means of fulfilling the "rights" of the recipient. Whether you rob a productive man from compassion or greed—from a desire to shower yourself or others with the unearned—whether perpetrated by an individual or a government—it is still robbery and a violation of the producer's rights.)

If society is to be a boon, not a hazard, to a man's life, it must recognize and protect his rights. This means that the individuals composing a society must create an agency capable of providing protection to men. Because a man's rights can be violated only by the initiation of physical force against him, that agency must have the authority and the power to restrain the force initiators. That agency, of course, is the government.[7]

It is only because rational men require protection from those who would initiate force or fraud against them that a government must be formed. A government, Ayn Rand trenchantly observes, is an agency holding a legal monopoly on the use of force within a specific geographical area. A proper government is constitutionally restricted from the *initiation of force*—and limited to its retaliatory use against those who do initiate it. In this regard, the Bill of Rights contained within the *United States Constitution* is an epoch-making document. Whatever its omissions or shortcomings, its guarantee of American citizens' basic rights, and its legal prohibition of any government's action to violate them, is a historic attempt to eliminate government's power to initiate force.

The initiation of force can be terminated only by the ability and willingness to use superior force in retaliation against it. Force initiators demonstrate, by means of their own choices and actions, that they have placed themselves outside the bounds of rational persuasion. The police cannot reason with violent criminals, for example; they must, in part, deploy superior force to apprehend or kill them. Similarly, the only factor that protected the lives and freedom of untold millions of human beings against the murderous aggression of Hitler and Stalin was the overpowering military might of America and her allies, and their willingness to use it to defend themselves.

A proper government bans the initiation of force from men's lives. In effect, a government constitutionally limited to the protection of individual rights—and thereby debarred from violating them—places the use of force entirely under the control of reason. For one thing, force will be used only for a rational purpose; it will never be initiated, but will be employed only in retaliation against the initiators. This means that men's right to guide their lives by means of their own thinking will be legally protected. Such a government is the upholder and defender of each individual's right to live as a rational being.

Second: even in retaliation, the use of force will be guided by rationally-arrived-at principles, i.e., laws. For example, the law will require the police to show a judge evidence that an individual is engaged in criminal activities before they would be permitted to search his premises or tap his phones. The law will require the police to use no more force than necessary to subdue a suspect or to protect their own safety. The penalty for specific crimes will be decided upon by means of carefully-reasoned moral and legal arguments—and attempt to achieve commensurability between transgression and punishment. The law will require the prosecution to provide conclusive evidence of the defendant's guilt before he could be convicted and sentenced to incarceration or execution. Etc.

A proper government prohibits a whim-based or emotionalist use of force, ensuring that its legal employment is always under the guidance of rational principles. Such a government, by virtue of consistently upholding individual rights, thereby safeguards each man's right to the unrestricted use of his own mind. *A proper government is the indispensable protective agency of the mind.*

Rationally construed, a government is an agency with one purpose: to protect individual rights. The implementation of this purpose involves three functions: a government must provide a criminal justice system, a system of civil courts that arbitrate legitimate disputes among honest men, and a (volunteer) military to defend the nation against foreign invaders.

Such a limited government would do more than provide the indispensable service of protecting men from criminals and militaristically aggressive nations, i.e., from force initiators of both the domestic and foreign varieties. It would also provide an impartial, legally binding forum in which the countless honest disputes among men are adjudicated and settled within the context of objective laws designed to protect the rights of each individual citizen. "Under such a system [of civil courts], none of the parties needs to (or may) decide unilaterally that he is a victim with the onus of taking physical action to repair his interests." Regarding the civil law also, the government, by protecting the rights of each individual, precludes the arbitrary initiation of force (by plaintiff or defendant) against the other. For example, if men sign an employment contract but later disagree regarding its interpretation, neither employer nor employee can legally use force as a means of redressing his specific grievance. In the absence of voluntary agreement on the part of the disputants, only the civil courts, as an impartial arbiter ruling in accordance with objectively-defined laws, can legally (and morally) resolve such a case. A civil court system is the most important function a government can provide, for "criminals are a small minority; [but] contractual protection for honest undertakings...is a daily necessity of civilized life."[8]

Today, some people believe that government, by its nature, is evil and that the protection of individual rights requires anarchy, i.e., the absence of government. A concretization of this theory illustrates the principle sufficient to refute it. Men need protection from both foreign enemies and criminals, as well as an objective means of arbitrating honest disagreements. In the absence of government, who protects the members of a free society from Nazis, Communists or Islamists? The answer: nobody. Would private citizens need to be ceaselessly armed or hire bodyguards to protect themselves from gangsters? In a word: yes. In the absence of governmental civil courts, could a deadbeat simply dismiss the judgment of a private arbitrator and renege with impunity on a signed contract or agreement? Again, yes.

A proper government holds a monopoly on the use of force and subordinates it to objective moral law. Lacking such an agency, honest men will have no means to legally enforce contracts or other agreements—they will exist in perennial danger from criminals—and they will be helpless before the armies of a conquering dictator. Such a society is immediately subjugated by foreign aggressors or its inevitable internal gang warfare results in the emergence of a dominant political "strongman." Either way, an anarchic society devolves quickly into dictatorship. Ultimately, anarchy is not a system of freedom but of its opposite: of statism. It is a brief provisional period of chaos before the curtain of full-blown dictatorship descends. The deeper reason is that anarchy is the political institutionalization of whim worship, emotionalism, and the personal version of the primacy of consciousness error in metaphysics.[9]

To understand the enormous value of a government dedicated to the protection of individual rights, it is necessary to examine it in light of the principles discussed earlier in this book. Values, we know, are the meaning of a man's life; indeed, a necessity of it; and values must be created by human effort. It follows that for a man to live and flourish, he must have a right to own the values created by his mind and effort. The principle of individual rights, including the right to property, protected and enforced by a constitutionally-limited government, is an indispensable necessity of such flourishing life.

Deeper, we saw that the requirements of human life form the standard of moral value. That which promotes man's life is the good, and that which harms or kills it is the evil. Measured by this standard, the principle of individual rights is an enormous, unqualified good; for when men's rights are recognized and protected, all men can thrive; but when they are not, in principle, no man can. For men to live, they must have the moral, legally-protected right to live. For men to live, each man must have the right to his own life.

In terms of the book's theme, such protection of men's rights leaves free every rational member of society to live by his own mind. It is not the case that such a society can guarantee men will be rational; given the volitional nature of human consciousness, it is always possible that some individuals will choose to abjure their minds. It does, however, guarantee that those who do choose ration- ality will be free to exercise it—and those who do not will be legally constrained in their attempt to initiate force or fraud against the rational producers. The pro- tection of individual rights liberates mankind's survival instrument—so it is no historical accident that the freest nations are those in which more men survive, i.e., have the highest living standards and longest life expectancies. The men of the mind need safety from the men of brute force—and the principle of individ- ual rights, fully understood and conscientiously upheld, provides it. *The princi- ple of individual rights protects the ability of the men of the mind to lead ra- tional lives.* Once again, from a new perspective, The Lesson of Objectivism is observed.

Logically and historically, the only political-economic system upholding the principle of individual rights is: capitalism. Although its nature has generally been distorted, misunderstood, and misrepresented by generations of critics, both secular and religious, it is to it that men owe the unprecedented freedom and prosperity currently enjoyed in the Western world. As will be seen next, Ayn Rand finally provided the moral and philosophical validation of capitalism that men desperately need to learn.

Chapter 12

Capitalism as the System Embodying
Rational Philosophical Principles

The nature (and the history) of capitalism have been egregiously distorted by Marxist and other anti-capitalist intellectuals. But capitalism's essence can be stated succinctly: capitalism is the system that protects the inalienable right of each individual to his own life. As Ayn Rand put it: "Capitalism is a social system based on the recognition of individual rights, including property rights, in which all property is privately owned."[1]

The essence of the capitalist system is a limited government which protects the rights of each individual to live by his own judgment in all areas of life, including both personal morality and economics (this implies, of course, that each individual must respect the rights of all other individuals). Such a system guarantees individuals freedom of speech, of the press—indeed, of all forms of intellectual expression—of religion, and of voting. Human beings are free to earn and to own property—their own homes, farms, and land. They are free to start their own businesses and to retain the profits that they earn. Capitalism provides a rule of law that protects private property, safeguards investments, and enforces contractual agreements. The overarching principle is: capitalism is the system of individual rights.

Ayn Rand emphasizes the right to own property. The underlying philosophical reason is that man is a composite of mind and body. It has been shown in Chapter Four that the mind is man's survival instrument, the fundamental means by which he creates the values required by his life. *But he lives a physical existence.* One point demonstrated in Chapter Eleven is that a man's bodily life is impossible to sustain in the absence of his right to the material values he creates. Life is, as Ayn Rand defines it, "a process of self-sustaining and self-generated action." Part of such ongoing activity is the need to create the food, clothing, shelter, medical care, transportation, communication, etc., upon which the furthering of a man's life depends. If he does not possess the legally-protected right to retain the wealth he creates, then any brute, burglar or—worst of all—dictatorial government can seize it at whim, leaving him to starve or freeze. *There is no right to life in the absence of a right to property*[2]

One consequence of an individual's inalienable right to private property is that each man has the right to dispose of the values he produces in any manner he deems appropriate. All re-distribution of property requires the owner's voluntary consent; no re-distribution may properly occur in the absence of such consent. This means that each individual has the right to engage in trade with other individuals—transactions undertaken by mutual consent and to mutual advantage. The initiation of force by either private individuals or the government itself is legally banned; the theft or coercive re-distribution of property is legally prohibited; and so men are free to live by what Ayn Rand terms the "trader principle": giving value for value in a free exchange of material products, ideas or any other human good. Such protection of the rights to property and voluntary trade—and the outlawing of initiated force—constitutes a moral prerequisite of civilized society.

Economically, the only system consonant with individual rights is: laissez-faire capitalism. The French term "laissez-faire" stands for a political-economic system in which the government "keeps its hands off" the life, rights, and mind of each and every non-criminal individual. The full legal separation of state and economy achieved under the principles of laissez-faire (and only under such principles) means elimination of *governmental initiation of coercion* from the realm in which men create and exchange the goods and services upon which their lives depend. (Indeed, more broadly, it means the eradication of governmental *initiation* of coercion from every aspect of an individual's life.)

In economics, as generally, the government's proper role is to protect individual rights; i.e., to provide civil courts to uphold contractual agreements among honest men—and to prosecute, by means of a system of criminal justice, those who willfully initiate force or fraud. If a businessman commits a criminal act, if he initiates force or fraud against any individual—whether a competitor, colleague, shareholder, employee or anyone else—then he should be prosecuted to the fullest extent of the law, regardless of his wealth (or lack of it). Beyond such protection of individual rights, the government has no role to play in the economy. Near the end of *Atlas Shrugged*, one of the heroes, a judge, adds a clause to the *U.S. Constitution* that is consistent with its basic principle of individual rights: "Congress shall make no law abridging the freedom of production and trade." The governmental policy of "laissez-faire" or non-interventionism constitutes the consistent application of the broader principle of individual rights in the field of economics.[3]

By now, the reasons for a laissez-faire economic system should be clear. The production and voluntary exchange of commodities and services is an unqualified good, for human life depends on it. (See Chapter Eight.) Producing values, and freely trading them, is a requirement of man's survival—and, as such, is a major moral virtue. (See Chapter Nine.) If men have an inalienable right to their own lives—which includes the right to their own minds and bodies—then it follows that they have the right to the effort of their minds and bodies, and to retain the product of such effort. This means, of course, the right of individuals to own property, to start their own businesses or farms, to seek profit, and to retain their earnings. (See Chapter Eleven.) Such selfish economic activity is enormously beneficial to man's life. Consequently, it is a practice to be intransigently protected.

For example, commercial success in such fields as steelmaking, clothing design and manufacturing, the creation of software, etc., is as positive and life promoting as is practicing heart surgery, writing novels, composing symphonies or gaining theoretical scientific knowledge. None of these pursuits are immoral, much less criminal, and are to be neither restricted nor penalized by law. The conclusion therefore is: Those who initiate force or fraud should be punished. Those who respect men's rights should be protected. Those who create wealth in any field should gain and retain their earnings.

Statists (i.e., those who advocate governmental initiation of force in any form) deride the laissez-faire system as "do-nothing" government. This is utterly false and misleading. First, the government of a free society protects the right to life of every individual citizen—a monumentally important and on-going function, and one possible only to the government. This is hardly a "do-nothing" task. To avoid any misunderstanding: laissez-faire means that the government is legally prohibited from *initiating* force—but is legally obligated to employ *retaliatory* force against any and all private citizens who initiate it. Laissez-faire means constitutionally limited government, not anarchy.

Second: by protecting the rights of every individual, the laissez-faire state liberates men to create values—to innovate and invent, to build homes, farms and factories, to start their own companies, to create works of art, music, and literature, to originate theories in philosophy and science, i.e., to produce the incalculable material and spiritual wealth so characteristic of free societies. So-called "do-nothing" government makes possible a society of "free to do" rational individuals, of "do-much" productive citizens, who have made Western Europe, the United States, and the Asian Tigers the wealthiest nations of history. (The governments of these nations are mixed economies, not laissez-faire systems, i.e., they are mixtures of freedom and statism, of individual rights and collectivism, of capitalism and socialism. But the element of freedom is dominant in all of them, making possible the explosion of creativity by private, often profit-seeking individuals and companies so characteristic of capitalist societies.)

Governmental intervention in the economy always involves the initiation of physical force, i.e., it inevitably violates individual rights—often those of highly productive men. For example: the practice of eminent domain enables the government to seize a man's land or home against his will. Despite paying the owner "fair market value," such a policy constitutes an egregious violation of his rights; for the government takes no cognizance of whether the owner thinks the trade is "fair,"—i.e., beneficial to him—and *chooses* to sell; rather, it compels him to.

A mixed economy is a product of a "mixed-up" government, i.e., a confused farrago of legislation mixing laws that protect individual rights with those that violate them. In direct opposition to its proper role as protector of innocent men from criminals, the state then becomes, in numerous instances, a criminal. For example, the Internal Revenue Service is legally empowered to rob men—and the more productive the man, the higher the percentage of his income it robs. Another case in point: the government, in many industries, *forces* companies to negotiate with labor unions; it does not permit them to hire independent, non-union workers—and imposes the corollary of such a policy, coercively prohibiting non-union men from working for those companies. Such a policy, of course, violates the right of both the company to hire whomever will voluntarily work for it—and that of an independent worker to gain employment from whomever chooses to hire him.

As yet another example: anti-trust legislation prohibits productive companies from gaining a market share the government deems excessive—in spite of the fact that, under the policy of laissez-faire, a huge market share is gained in open competition only by winning the voluntary patronage of millions of customers. The government coercively breaks up companies it considers too successful, i.e., too productive. By means of such an unjust policy, the government tramples the rights of producers, and, as a consequence, abrogates the rights of millions of customers to voluntarily patronize the companies they prefer.

(The coercive, destructive monopolies that men properly fear, e.g., the "Big Four" of 19th century railroad infamy, are always established by means of governmental intervention in the economy. The key factor making possible a coercive monopoly is *closed entry* to the marketplace; that is, the government provides one firm with an exclusive franchise and legally debars would-be competitors from entering the field. Such an abrogation of laissez-faire was the root cause of the Big Four's ruinous power—and that of any similar monopolist. The implementation of laissez-faire obviates the problem, for then a "monopolist" has no power to legally restrict competitors from entering the field.)[4]

Numerous other instances can be adduced, but the principle is clear: governmental intervention in the economy, always and everywhere, involves the initiation of force against innocent, often enormously productive men. In a mixed economy, the government's police power is deployed both *in retaliation* against criminals—and *in initiation* against peaceful men. This means that, at the same time, in different respects, the government both protects and violates the rights of innocent men.

The capitalist revolution, initiated in Great Britain at the turn of the 19th century, although not fully consistent, brought what constituted, at that time, the greatest protection of individual rights in human history. This meant that *the government's legal initiation of force was at its historic all-time low.* The result was that men were liberated, to the greatest extent thus far of history, to live egoistically—to pursue their own values, their own success, their own happiness—and to employ their rational thinking, virtually without restriction, to do so. What followed, as the principles of a rational philosophy predict, was an explosion of rational creativity in the sciences, the arts, technology, medicine, and industrialization—all of it leading to historically unprecedented living standards and life expectancies.

A brief history of capitalism reveals the enormity of progress it has achieved. Great Britain, during the 18th and early 19th centuries, was the first European nation to throw off the oppression of feudalism and monarchy and begin to institute a system of individual rights. Also during this period, Britain's North American colonies fomented a historic revolution that established the freest country of history. In the 19th century, the ideals of individualism, limited government, and capitalism gradually spread to most of the nations of Western Europe, leading to the overthrow of the *ancien regime*. For the next 100 years, freedom and capitalism existed exclusively in Western Europe and North America.

What were the results? One economist, Angus Maddison, estimated that in Europe in 1700 per capita income was roughly $265. Most European nations were akin to Africa today—desperately-poor, famine-ridden countries. (Indeed, they were far poorer; for at least in Africa today there accrue some of the benefits of modern medicine, agriculture, electricity, automobiles, airplanes, computers and the Internet, etc. But these are products of the capitalist era—generally of America—and did not yet exist in the 18th century.) This point goes far to explain a European life expectancy of that period that did not reach thirty-five years.[5]

But Britain's Technological and Industrial Revolutions of the late 18th and 19th centuries brought enormous progress. For the first time in centuries, the minds of common men were freed from bondage to the feudal aristocracy and the established religion; free to ask and answer scientific questions, to apply newly-discovered principles to practical concerns, to invent technologies, to industrialize, and to manufacture vastly-increased supplies of consumer goods.

James Watt (1736-1819), as one outstanding example, perfected the steam engine, the "Work Engine of the Industrial Revolution," which immeasurably increased men's ability to manufacture the goods their lives required. Edward Jenner (1749-1823), created a vaccine for smallpox, one of history's deadliest diseases. George Stephenson (1781-1848), pioneered the design of locomotives for use on the newly-developing railroads. All of these thinkers and many more were commoners whose minds and activities would have been stifled under the *ancien regime* that continued to hold sway on the European Continent. It was Britain's far greater political-economic freedom that provided the social conditions her most innovative minds needed to create unprecedented material progress.

In the 19th century—based on the advances in applied science, technology, industry, medicine, and agriculture made possible by the protection of men's right to live egoistically and by the resultant liberation of the human mind—the standard of living increased dramatically; the life expectancy rose from the low-thirties that held under the pre-capitalist systems; moreover, Europe's population roughly tripled. In Britain, the freest European nation, per capita living standards rose during the 19th century while the population more than tripled. For example, British real wages in the decades of 1781-1851—income measured in terms of purchasing power, of what individuals can buy with their money—showed an average increase in excess of 60 percent for farm workers, over 86 percent for blue collar workers, and more than 140 percent for all workers, including white collar ones. One practical result of such rise in real income was the end of the ages-old practice of child labor—for now mother and father were able to support their offspring without the need for the children to provide income.[6]

In the United States, economic progress was even more dramatic. Capitalism and the Technological/Industrial Revolutions reached their full fruition there in the late-19th century. Advances such as Cyrus McCormick's reaper, Samuel Morse's telegraph, Alexander Graham Bell's telephone, Thomas Edison's electric lighting system, Henry Ford's mass production of automobiles, the Wright brothers' airplane, and numerous other devices helped establish America as the most progressive and wealthiest society of history. Per capita living standards doubled between 1790 and 1860, and then doubled again between 1865 and 1915—this at a time when the country absorbed millions of destitute immigrants from Ireland, Sicily, and Eastern Europe. America's unprecedented productivity, led by such giants of industry as Andrew Carnegie, John D. Rockefeller, and James J. Hill, kept American output so far ahead of population growth that the country's high living standards became legendary as early as the turn of the 20th century.[7]

Part of the productivity brought about by capitalism was that famine—the scourge of all non-capitalist systems both historically and currently—was wiped out in the free world. Advances in both agricultural science and technology are responsible for the enormous abundance of food produced in America and the other Western countries. *There has never been a famine in the history of the United States.* The author's research could not discover a famine in the history of any capitalist nation. The significance of this is too often overlooked: in less than a century, capitalism proved mistaken the Malthusian doctrine that population growth inevitably outstrips food production. Malthus is tragically correct, however, regarding all non-capitalist societies.

Currently, the system of individual rights is responsible for all global advances in freedom and prosperity. The countries of Western (and today Central) Europe, North America, and the "Asian Tigers"—e.g., Japan, Hong Kong, Taiwan—though hardly flawless, have, to some degree implemented the principle of individual rights. The logical consequence is that these are, politically, the freest nations of human history—and, economically, the wealthiest by many orders of magnitude.

By contrast, under any form of statism—be it feudalism, theocracy, Fascism, Communism, welfare state socialism, etc.—an individual's right to his own life, his pursuit of happiness, and his mind are abrogated to a greater or lesser degree. The state is pre-eminent; to some extent, each individual is morally obligated and legally coerced to serve it. Under such a ruling principle, the state can and does initiate force against its own citizens. Instead of serving as a protector of men's rights, a statist regime becomes the gravest threat to them. The best among men are restrained, not liberated; the worst are liberated, not restrained, i.e., the most heinous criminals, such mass murderers as Hitler, Stalin, and Mao, run the government. The men of the mind are enslaved; the men of brute force are empowered.

When men have no right to their lives, then it follows that they cannot live.

In countless forms, they die at the hands of the state. The government can expropriate their property, including the food they have grown, leaving them to die from massive famine—as under Stalin. Or: the government can construct vast extermination camps, then herd in millions of innocent human beings to be gassed to death—as under Hitler. Or: the government can draft into its military thousands of young men to wage endless wars of conquest against neighboring states, raining death and enslavement on foreign populations, as well as on its own—as under Saddam Hussein and an endless litany of bloodthirsty regimes throughout history.

Even under a mixed economy, where men still possess some rights—as in the nations of the contemporary West—the government can steal a percentage of their income to provide for the poor (the welfare state); or prevent them from developing their own property (environmental restrictions); or force them to endure endless waiting periods for medical treatment—even unnecessary death—because the private practice of medicine has been banned or at least greatly curtailed by law (socialized medicine); etc. A mixed economy is a chaotic farrago of more than differing economic systems: it is a mixture of moral, political, and economic principles—of egoism and altruism, of individualism and collectivism, of freedom and statism, of capitalism and socialism, i.e., of nutritious food and poison.

For all the reasons described in this book, it is the principle of freedom, not that of government controls, that is responsible for the prosperity of the mixed economies. The wealth of Americans, for example, would rise, not fall, if governmental restrictions on the productive activities of rational men were lifted. Indeed, if statism rather than freedom were responsible for generating widespread prosperity, it follows that the former Soviet Union and its socialist satellites would have been wealthy, and the United States and its semi-capitalist allies destitute—but empirically, the exact opposite was (and remains) true.

The contrasting economic results of capitalism and statism—the differences between governmental protection of men's rights and its violation of them—are manifest. The freest nations of the world are vastly wealthier than those politically repressed; indeed, they enjoy per capita incomes four to ten times that of the statist regimes. As but one example: individuals trapped in Castro's Cuba earn a mere fraction of the wealth enjoyed by their countrymen a scant 100 miles away in Miami.[8]

The explanatory principles should be clear. At the political level, it can be concluded that the government, as an institution of force, is incapable of production, for the latter involves the creative power of man's mind, i.e., the antithesis of physical coercion. *Government can be protective, but not productive*: by using force only in retaliation against those who initiate it, a proper government provides a physical haven for the best members of mankind—those who choose to think—against the brutes, thereby safeguarding their creative faculties. But the government's physical restraint of criminals and foreign aggressors is not itself creative.

At the ethical level: when men have the right to live and pursue happiness, then the moral principle of egoism is legally protected. Men's need and desire to create values is sanctioned, encouraged, and rewarded—therefore, the enormous value creation under capitalism. But under statism, by contrast, men have right to neither their lives nor the pursuit of happiness, and the principle of egoism is legally abrogated. The enormous creative power arising from men's need and fervent desire to create values is thereby expunged from human life. The creation of values is severed from the use and enjoyment of values—and the motivation to produce them is severely undercut.

Therefore, we arrive at several philosophical conclusions. The first point explaining capitalism's enormous life-giving success is: the principle of individual rights protects men's ability to live egoistically, i.e., to create and retain the values that their survival requires. This is the fundamental moral reason that capitalism creates such widespread abundance.

This point is true spiritually, as well as materially. Under capitalism, men hold the legally-protected right to create intellectual, artistic, and spiritual values, as well as material ones. For example, philosophers, writers, artists, musicians, scientists, and theoreticians of every variety enjoy the same freedoms as do entrepreneurs, inventors, technologists, and industrialists. Consequently, a publishing industry flourishes in the capitalist nations, creating books and articles of every kind; similarly regarding a music industry; and art museums and galleries proliferate in every major city. Thinkers teach, lecture, and publish on every conceivable topic, presenting every imaginable viewpoint. Men's lives require ideas, knowledge, and art just as much as they do food—indeed, such intellectual advances provide an indispensable foundation for men's ability to create a plentiful supply of food and other material values—and it is the principle of individual rights that protects their right to create them.

The second conclusion is that capitalism is the system of the mind—the only system that unleashes and maximizes creative human brain power. When men are free to create values, they are free to employ their instrument of creating values—their mind. When human beings possess the legally-protected right to unrestrictedly employ their survival instrument, then they will survive in greater numbers, in greater comfort, and for greater periods of time. This is the deepest epistemological reason that capitalism creates such widespread abundance. Ayn Rand's unrestricted endorsement of laissez-faire capitalism follows logically from her unqualified endorsement of man's mind—and represents, in a new form, The Lesson of Objectivism.

Politically, epistemologically, and morally, capitalism emerges triumphant.

Politically, capitalism is the only system to recognize and protect an individual's inalienable right to his own life, which means: the right to employ his mind in service of his life. Therefore, *epistemologically*, capitalism is the system of liberated, unrestrained rationality. Related: rationality is man's cardinal virtue; therefore, *morally*, capitalism is the system making possible the full, unrestricted practice of virtue. Further, since the virtue of rationality is the primary means by which men create values, capitalism is the system of unparalleled value achievement.

Because of the points discussed so far in this book, it is possible to sum up capitalism's life-giving nature and unrivalled success: *it is the sole social-*

economic system embodying rational philosophical principles.

Epilogue:

The Lesson of Objectivism Re-Stated

We have now gone through, in terms of essentials, the full corpus of the Objectivist system of thought, and numerous principles have been identified. The Lesson of Objectivism can now be comprehended in greater detail.

Values are the meaning of life—and for X to be of value its (or his) nature or actions must be congruent with the *factual* requirements of man's survival. Any entity, action or relationship that is harmful to man's *objective* survival requirements is thereby disqualified from the realm of values.

Related, Ayn Rand holds that *rationality* is the sole means of achieving values. The very theme of *Atlas Shrugged* is that the *rational mind* is mankind's survival instrument—and the abrogation of its requirements, in any form, for any motive, means that men will not be able to survive.

Further, the heroic potential of every man is based on a willingness to inviolably support and uphold life-promoting values. In her greatest novels, characters of modest intellectual ability, such as Mike Donnigan and Eddie Willers, are shown to be as fully committed to the *factual* requirements of man's life as are the great geniuses. Heroism, Ayn Rand shows, is an unswerving commitment to *rationality*, regardless of intellectual ability.

Rationality is consequently man's supreme virtue, the fundamental character trait enabling human beings to achieve every value on which their lives depend. The subsidiary virtues are all applications of *rationality* in specific contexts.

Happiness, the proper goal of every *rational* man's life, is the result of achieving values, and can be attained only by a consistent commitment to *rationality*, man's survival instrument, i.e., his value-achieving instrument.

Individuals possess inalienable rights, because these are a requirement of a *rational* being's survival. For an individual to survive, he must act in accordance with the judgments of his survival instrument; and consequently, the means of preventing his doing so—the initiation of force—must be outlawed. The prin-

117

ciple of individual rights is a necessary means of securing a *rational* being's ability to create values, i.e., to live.

A proper government is, consequently, dedicated and limited to the protection of individual rights. Laissez-faire capitalism, the political-economic system that achieves this purpose, is, therefore, the sole system consonant with the moral principle necessitated by the requirements of a *rational* being's survival. Capitalism is the system that protects men's ability to live by *the mind.* It is the system of *rationality.* It is the system of virtue. It is the system of values.

Underlying and making possible these truths is the principle that the universe is an *intelligible* natural system in which existence holds primacy over consciousness, in which every existent is identified, and in which action flows necessarily from each entity's identity. In a world devoid of miracles or any other violation of the universal principles of identity and causality, knowledge is gained only by a *rational,* i.e., an *objective* method—only by consciousness recognizing and adhering to the primacy of existence principle.

Condensed to essentials, this means: values, that which makes man's life possible and meaningful, are gained solely by rationality. Objectively, gaining values is the good; any form of sacrificing them is evil. The achievement of values requires that men be left free to act on their rational judgment. This is the basis of the moral principle of individual rights: each man's inalienable right to his own life necessitates his right to live by his own mind. Limited Constitutional government—capitalism—is the sole system to protect men's rights to their own lives and minds, and is, therefore, the only moral system. Underlying this, reason is the sole means of efficaciously dealing with reality because of the primacy of existence: the mind must identify facts, and comprehend and obey nature's laws; it cannot create or control them.

This is an amplified expression of the Lesson of Objectivism: In every issue and moment of life, reason is the sole means by which human beings gain knowledge, values, and happiness.

Endnotes

These abbreviations have been employed for books that are frequently referenced:

AS	*Atlas Shrugged*
The FH	*The Fountainhead*
CUI	*Capitalism the Unknown Ideal*
FNI	*For the New Intellectual*
OPAR	*Objectivism: the Philosophy of Ayn Rand*
PWNI	*Philosophy Who Needs It*
VoR	*The Voice of Reason*
VoS	*The Virtue of Selfishness*

1: Why Philosophy?

1. Jonathan Hughes, *The Vital Few: American Economic Progress and its Protagonists* (Boston, Mass.: Houghton Mifflin, 1966), pp. 149-213.
2. www.crimelibrary.com/gangsters
3. Ayn Rand, *PWNI*, pp. 2-3.
4. *Ibid*, p. 3.
5. *Ibid.*, p. 4.
6. *Ibid.*, p. 2. *OPAR*, p. 2.
7. *PWNI*, p. 6.

2: Values as the Meaning of Life

1. *The FH*, pp. 307-08.
2. *Ibid.*, pp. 335-36.
3. *VoS*, p. 15.
4. *The FH*, pp. 194-97.
5. *Ibid.*, p. 49.
6. *VoS*, pp. 50-6.
7. *AS*, p. 1030.

3: Egoism vs. Cynical Exploitativeness

1. *AS*, p. 731.
2. *OPAR* , pp. 234-36. *The FH*, pp. 604-08. *VoS*, pp. vii-xi.
3. *The FH*, p. 355. *VoS*, p. ix.
4. *The FH*, p. 679.

4: Rationality as Man's Means of Survival

1. *The FH*, p. 679.
2. *AS*, pp. 782-83.
3. *The FH*, p. 679.
4. *AS*, pp. 1012-14.
5. *Ibid.*, pp. 1017-18.

5: The Universe as an Intelligible Natural System

1. *OPAR*, pp. 4-5.
2. *AS*, p. 1016.
3. *OPAR*, pp. 6-7.
4. *Ibid.*, p. 14.
5. *AS*, p. 1015.
6. *Ibid.*, p. 1015.
7. *OPAR*, p. 18.
8. *AS*, p. 1016.
9. *OPAR*, p. 18.
10. *The FH*, p. 24.
11. Paul Johnson, *Modern Times* (New York: HarperPerennial, 1992), p. 546.
12. *PWNI*, pp. 28-41. *OPAR*, pp. 23-30.

6: Objectivity as the Method of Rational Cognition

1. *VoR*, p. 18.
2. *Ibid.*, p. 18.
3. *OPAR*, p. 116.
4. *Ibid.*, pp. 116-18.
5. *AS*, pp. 1016-17.
6. *OPAR*, p. 119.
7. Niles Eldredge, *The Triumph of Evolution and the Failure of Creationism* (New York: W.H. Freeman and Co., 2000.), pp. 32-60.
8. Andrew Bernstein, *The Capitalist Manifesto: The Historic, Philosophic, and Economic Case for Laissez-Faire* (Lanham, Md.: University Press of America, 2005), pp. 29-161.
9. Henry Hazlitt, *Economics In One Lesson* (Westport, Ct.: Arlington House, 1979.) Ludwig von Mises, *Human Action: A Treatise on Economics*, third revised edition (Chicago: Henry Regnery, 1966); *idem.*, *Socialism* (Indianapolis, Indiana: Liberty Fund, 1981).
10. Stephane Courtois, et. al., *The Black Book of Communism: Crimes, Terror, Repression.* (Cambridge, Mass.: 1999), *passim.*
11. *OPAR*, p. 117.
12. *Ibid.*, p. 117.

7: Man the Hero

1. *AS*, p. 1012.
2. *Ibid.*, p. 1012.
3. *Ibid.*, p. 1013.
4. *The FH*, pp. 677-685.

8: The Nature of the Good

1. *VoS.*, pp. 13-4.
2. *Ibid.*, p. 16.
3. *Ibid.*, pp. 16-7.
4. *OPAR*, pp. 192-93.
5. *VoS*, pp. 15-16.
6. *AS*, p. 1013.

7. *VoS*, p. 23.
8. *Ibid.*, p. 27. *The FH*, p. 679.

9: Virtue as a Requirement of Survival

1. *OPAR*, p. 250.
2. *VoS*, p. 26.
3. *OPAR*, p. 255.
4. *The FH*, p. 261.
5. *Ibid.*, p. 241.
6. *VoS*, p. 69. *AS*, p. 1019.
7. *VoS*, p. 26. *AS*, p. 1019.
8. *OPAR*, pp. 267-68.
9. *Ibid.*, p. 270.
10. *Ibid.*, pp. 270-71.
11. *Ibid.*, p. 271.
12. *Ibid.* pp. 271-72. *AS*, p. 1019.
13. *AS*, p. 1019.
14. *OPAR*, pp. 276, 278.
15. *VoS*, p. 72.
16. *OPAR*, p. 285.
17. *Ibid.*, pp. 290-91.
18. *VoS*, p. 26.
19. *FNI*, p. 15.
20. *OPAR*, p. 294.
21. *AS*, p. 1020.
22. *OPAR*, p. 304.
23. *Ibid.*, p. 307.
24. *Ibid.*, pp. 305-06.

10: The Moral and the Practical

1. *OPAR*, pp. 326-27.
2. *Ibid.*, p. 337.
3. *AS*, p. 1022.
4. *Ibid.*, pp. 959-60.
5. *OPAR*, p. 341.
6. *Ibid.*, p. 341.
7. *Ibid.*, p. 342.
8. *Ibid.*, p. 342.
9. *Ibid.*, p. 342.

11: Individual Rights and Government

1. *OPAR*, p. 352.
2. *AS*, p. 1023.
3. *VoS*, pp. 92-3.
4. *OPAR*, pp. 351-52.
5. *VoS*, p. 94.
6. *AS*, p. 1061.
7. *OPAR*, p. 363.

8. *Ibid.*, p. 366.
9. *VoS*, pp. 112-13. *OPAR*, pp. 371-73.

12: Capitalism—the System of the Mind

1. *CUI*, p. 19.
2. *VoS*, p. 15.
3. *AS*, pp. 1167-68.
4. *CUI*, pp. 102-109. Oscar Lewis, *The Big Four* (New York: Alfred Knopf, 1938), *passim.*
5. Angus Maddison, *Phases of Capitalist Development* (New York: Oxford University Press, 1982), pp. 4-7. Andrew Bernstein, *The Capitalist Manifesto: The Historic, Economic, and Philosophic Case for Laissez-Faire* (Lanham, Md.: University Press of America, 2005), pp. 55-72, 103-36.
6. J. H. Clapham, *An Economic History of Modern Britain*, vol. 1, *The Early Railway Age* (Cambridge: Cambridge University Press, 1926), pp. 548-61. Peter Lindert and Jeffrey Williamson, "English Workers' Living Standards During the Industrial Revolution: A New Look," *The Economic History Review*, 2nd Series, 36 (Feb. 1983), 1-2, 4-7, 23-24. Jeffrey Williamson, *Did British Capitalism Create Inequality* (Boston: Allen and Unwin, 1985), pp. 7-33. Clark Nardinelli, *Child Labor and the Industrial Revolution* (Bloomington, Ind.: Indiana University Press, 1990), pp. 108-10, 144, 149, 156.
7. Rondo Cameron, *A Concise Economic History of the World* (Oxford: Oxford University Press, 1997), p. 228. *The Vital Few, op. cit.*, p. 215.
8. Gerald O'Driscoll, et. al., *The 2001 Index of Economic Freedom* (Washington, DC: the Heritage Foundation and the *Wall Street Journal*, 2001), pp. 1-5. *The Capitalist Manifesto, op. cit.*, pp. 293-332.

Bibliography

The major books by and about Ayn Rand are as follows. This brief annotated bibliography does not represent a full list of works by or about Ayn Rand and her ideas, but is a good starting point for the beginning student.

Fiction

Ayn Rand, *Anthem* (New York: Signet), 1961. A novelette showing a future collectivist-dictatorship's regression into primitivism, and the re-discovery of the self by an innovative thinker.

Ayn Rand, *Atlas Shrugged* (New York: Plume, 1999). One of the great novels in world literature: dramatizes the catastrophic consequences for the world when the men of the mind go on strike against the altruist-collectivist moral creed dominating society.

Ayn Rand, *The Fountainhead* (New York: Penguin, 1993). A powerful story of an innovative architect's struggle to build and live independently in a conservative society dominated by entrenched beliefs hostile to him.

Ayn Rand, *We the Living* (New York: Signet, 1960.) Ayn Rand's semi-autobiographical first novel tells the gripping story of a heroic young woman and the two men who love her to lead independent lives under the crushing dictatorship of Soviet Russia.

Non-Fiction

Ayn Rand, *Capitalism the Unknown Ideal* (New York: Signet, 1967). A series of essays offering a revolutionary theory of capitalism's nature and history.

Ayn Rand, *Philosophy Who Needs It* (New York: Bobbs-Merrill, 1982). The title essay explains that and why all human beings need philosophy to guide their lives.

Ayn Rand, *For the New Intellectual* (New York: Signet, 1963). The title essay shows the role of philosophy in shaping the course of human history.

Ayn Rand, *The Romantic Manifesto* (New York: Signet, 1971). A detailed and incisive defense of the Romantic school of art.

Ayn Rand, *The Voice of Reason: Essays in Objectivist Thought* (New York: Meridian, 1990). A collection of essays on philosophy, culture, and politics by Ayn Rand and other leading Objectivist thinkers.

Ayn Rand, *The Virtue of Selfishness* (New York: Signet, 1964). In the lead essay, "The Objectivist Ethics," Ayn Rand provides a superb analysis of the essentials of her moral theory.

About Ayn Rand's Philosophy

Leonard Peikoff, *Objectivism: the Philosophy of Ayn Rand* (New York: Meridian, 1993). The definitive, systematic presentation of Ayn Rand's philosophy by her leading student and intellectual heir.

Allan Gotthelf, *On Ayn Rand* (Belmont, California: Wadsworth, 2000). A succinct and effective introduction to Ayn Rand's thought by a leading contemporary Aristotle scholar.

About The Author

Andrew Bernstein holds a Ph.D. in Philosophy from the Graduate School of the City University of New York. He teaches at Marist College and the State University of New York at Purchase, the latter of which selected him its Outstanding Faculty Member for 2004. His book, *The Capitalist Manifesto: The Historic, Economic and Philosophic Case for Laissez-Faire* was published in 2005 by University Press of America. His website is www.andrewbernstein.net